Tiaras and T-Shirts

Tiaras and T-Shirts

Muriel Arnold

Librario

Published by

Librario Publishing Ltd.

ISBN 10:   1-904440-92-4
ISBN 13:   978-1904440-92-5

Copies can be ordered via the Internet
www.librario.com

or from:

Brough House, Milton Brodie, Kinloss
Moray IV36 2UA
Tel/Fax No 00 44 (0)1343 850 178

Printed and bound by 4edge Ltd, Hockley. www.4edge.co.uk

Typeset by 3btype.com

For my neices, nephews and 'greats'

Jennifer · John · Christine · Bryan · Ashley · Sophie · Edward

Richard · Karen · Kevin

Isobel · Robert · Glenn · Zoë

Bridget · Daniel · Carolina · Indiana · Jerome

Margaret · Robin · Emily · Ryan · Lewis · Phoebe · Ted · Alice

Heather · Paul · Matthew · Naomi · Jacob · Beatrice · Joe

Pat · Tony · Luke · Sam

... travel is the greatest education in the world and if a gift could be bestowed upon a child I would choose curiosity.

Lillian Gish
on board *Queen Elizabeth 2*
30th March 1977

Contents

List of Illustrations

Foreword

by Commodore R W Warwick OBE

When Muriel Arnold first set foot on the *Queen Elizabeth* in the 1960's she became one of the few females to be employed at sea. It is therefore not surprising that very few words have been written by lady officers to recording their recollections and perspective of shipboard life.

During those early years Muriel lived a rather glamorous life attending to the desires of famous people whose only way to travel was by ship. Although she did not live the deprived life of a sailor billeted in the bows of the ship, she did have to endure ocean crossings on a liner without stabilizers and air conditioning, without computers and word processors. On the plus side there were more days in port and with it the opportunity to explore the exciting countries visited. Although the ships, the names and the faces may have changed today, life onboard has largely remained the same. This book is an accurate account of life then, which resembles a crew member's life today – they still work hard and play hard!

With a sharp eye for detail and vivid recollections, Audrey's diaries provide an important and historical record of a Lady Pursers busy life at sea in an era before typewriters and carbon paper became things of the past. From *Tiaras to T-Shirts* we are given a glimpse of life on board for the passengers, and an insight into the author's life aboard the gracious and fondly remembered Cunard liners, including the early years of the *Queen Elizabeth 2*.

Somerset – August 2007

Before The Mast

It is the first time I have worn a tiara. It isn't exactly heavy but I feel as if I must balance it all the time. The Queen doesn't seem to bat an eyelid – but then she's used to it.

I am sitting in a cream leather chair, wearing a plain black evening dress, in the brightly-lit Steiner Salon on board *Queen Elizabeth 2* staring at Mandy's reflection as she puts the finishing touches to this sparkling crown of diamonds nestling in my hair. She assures me that the tiara will stay in place. I am not so sure.

We are on a world cruise, en route from New York to Rio de Janeiro, with representatives from Roditi and Maximino Gems, two of Brazil's leading jewellers, on board. Shortly after sailing they booked every room available for lavish cocktail parties in the hope that the passengers will buy these fantastic jewels – emerald, aquamarine, tourmaline, diamond, amethyst, topaz. All mined in Brazil. Now they are staging a Fashion Show to raise the temperature of our elegant passengers.

A couple of days ago Roditi and Maximino were scouting for volunteer models – you, you and you. I was caught in their radar and consented to do my bit. Several other members of the staff had been recruited to model the jewels and, like me, are now being coiffured and adorned in the Salon.

Mandy stands back, satisfied that the tiara is sitting where it should and I am ready to be launched. The Security Officer, a man of late thirties with his clean-cut hair and bland good looks, watches as a diamond necklace is secured around my neck. Then a diamond bracelet is fastened to my left wrist and diamond earrings are clipped to my ears. Total value $140,000.

'Time to go,' he glances at his wristwatch and escorts me to the Queen's Room, stopping at the edge of the dance floor. A spotlight blinds me and I am aware of a dense concentration of passengers in the smoky gloom. Ladies in brightly coloured dresses, ivory shoulders with a blaze of jewels twinkling from necks, ears and fingers. But the dance floor looks like a skating rink. I step on to it gingerly and start to walk slowly round the floor as coquettishly as I can, moving my head from side to side, smiling into the darkness. I complete the circuit and as I step out of the spotlight there he is, the Security Officer, waiting for me!

I am baffled by the strong protection because I cannot think of any way in which the jewels can be stolen. We are deep sea, there is no gangway and no one can possibly escape with the jewels. But that Security Officer was never more than six inches from my side except when I walked around the dance floor.

Together we return to the Steiner Salon and I give up my spoils quietly. Now that I've done my bit there is a little more time to examine the jewellery. It is a matching suite, replica of a 13th-century Greek design. The tiara seems heavier on my head than in my hands – strange! I think I'm a poor choice for the tiara. It is magnificent but I think it would have looked better on a brunette. My hair is natural blonde – not enough contrast against those sparkling diamonds. But it is a fab experience, never to be repeated!

So what is a young woman from the back lanes of Lincolnshire doing on board the *Queen Elizabeth 2* strutting around the Queen's Room wearing a small fortune in diamond jewellery?

I had certainly come a long way. I was brought up on a lonely farm in Lincolnshire, a hamlet, with a sprinkling of houses amongst the fields and woods. I had one brother and two sisters and every day there would be a group of seven or eight children from these scattered houses galloping along the lanes to school in the nearest village, a mile and a half away.

Our satchels contained books and our dinner, carefully packed. Mother would make delicious individual pies (rabbit or chicken or beef) and we were each responsible for carrying our dinner safely, so not too much skylarking about with the gas masks please.

On arrival at school the small, oval earthenware dishes and the large washed potatoes, each carved with our initials, were handed in and someone, presumably the cook, would put them in the oven in time for dinner.

After school we would 'run a telewag and walk a telewag' – the distance between two telegraph poles – to quicken our pace home again. There are no telegraph poles now and the footpath is overgrown. No one walks to school along these lanes anymore.

We were a close-knit family with a wonderful father and mother, industrious and honest and caring. My father was what in those days was called Farm Foreman and rode about in a pony and trap. Today he would probably be called Farm Manager and ride about in a Land-Rover.

We were so lucky to have had an upbringing in rural Lincolnshire with acres of fields and woods to play in, brooks to dam and splash in, trees to climb, dens to make, haystacks to hide in, apples to scrump and we knew where the wild honeysuckle grew. The summer days seemed to be endless. In the winter we would take our sledges and ride down the Gulley, squealing and tumbling in the snow.

There was no shop for a mile and a half, no bus, no car, just our sturdy legs and our bikes. It made us very resourceful and of course, we grew up and left all this behind for ever. I didn't appreciate just how idyllic it had been until I was surrounded by forgotten, malnourished children in the slums around the world. Bombay and Cairo are vivid in my memory.

After Grantham Technical College I worked for Chartered Auctioneers and Estate Agents in Grantham but I wanted to know what was beyond Grantham.

Marconi's Wireless Telegraph Company was beyond Grantham with its Head Office in Chelmsford, and off I went. From there I was transferred to Marconi Española in Madrid as Translator.

It is now the Sixties and I am just back from Madrid with itchy feet. I am on the lookout for a job that will give me more travel. Quite by chance I spotted an article 'Women and the sea' in a glossy magazine, *Homes and Gardens*. The article warns that women who really want a seagoing career must be patient and persevering. Every company has a waiting list.

To enter the seagoing staff of Cunard as a Lady Assistant Purser candidates need secretarial experience at Director level and must pass shorthand, typing and language tests. I apply by letter and am summoned to Liverpool where Cunard have booked a room for me in the Adelphi Hotel – it is a two day ordeal. A short walk brings me to Cunard's Head Office on the waterfront but I am not in very good condition for the day ahead. I've slept badly and had been too nervous to eat much breakfast.

After a tour of this huge, gaunt building (affectionately known as The Kremlin) a plump, grey-haired lady with spectacles takes me into a small, stuffy office and dictates a technical paper at 120 words a minute. I can still remember a fragment of that test. It went something like this – 'the compression of globules of water on the ship's propeller creating...' and it got worse. I can hear her voice but I'm not getting it down. It is too difficult. My head is swimming and I'm hungry. It had been a big mistake not to eat breakfast. And I am nervous. And yes, I failed!

But this lady was a cosy, comfortable sort of person and clearly accustomed to failures. She explained that Cunard set a very high standard for entry and I would be given the opportunity to take the test again. Some weeks later I was back in Liverpool. Took the test and passed!

When I got to sea and swapped experiences with my shipmates I discovered that many of us failed that lousy shorthand paper on the first attempt.

The typing paper was at 65 w.p.m. and presented no problem. I also had oral examinations in French and Spanish. I was told that I needed to brush up my French.

Then I was ushered into a Board Room to appear before a row of sharp-suited Directors sitting at a long, polished table. They bombarded me with questions. I recorded some of them in my diary:

'Was I a good sailor?'

(Yes, if you count Dover – Calais and Vigo – Tilbury which includes Bay of Biscay)

'How much notice would I need to give?'

'One month'. (Already stated on application form)

'Why do you want to go to sea?'

'To travel and meet people'. (Already stated on application form)

I felt like a criminal. How dare I apply for such a job!

Next I had a medical examination. Then came the announcement. I was approved. My name would be placed on a waiting list and they would contact me when there was a vacancy. It was just a matter of waiting.

But it was an exciting time – waiting. There was a lot to do. Cunard sent me a long list of uniform requirements. We were responsible for buying everything. The uniform, the shirts, the tropical white dresses, shoes, epaulettes, Cunard buttons – and don't forget the hat! The uniform was identical to that of an Officer in the *Women's Royal Naval Service (WRNS)* and Cunard gave the names and addresses of recommended tailors. I chose Gieves of Bond Street. In for a penny... in for a pound!

I enjoyed my visits to Bond Street. The large oblong fitting room upstairs was lined with shelves stacked with neat slabs of superfine doeskin, barathea, lightweight serge. I chose barathea. It looked good for years.

Several half-clothed, head-less and legless Naval Officers stood around the room while the busy little tailor meticulously moulded the material into my uniform. I had several fittings and this is what my diary says: 'It is a maze of tackings and chalk but it's going to be wonderful.'

It consisted of a reefer jacket with eight gold-coloured buttons bearing the Cunard insignia. Our distinguishing braid on each sleeve was quarter of an inch of white velvet and half an inch of gold braid, precisely three inches from the cuff of the sleeve. Engineers wore purple (oil); Radio wore green (don't know why); Medical wore red (blood). The Navigating Officers wore no distinguishing braid, only gold and the Captain wore All Gold – lots of it.

With the reefer we wore a skirt with two pleats in front – essential for jumping over coamings, tripping up gangways, and tackling segregation gates between First, Cabin and Tourist Class! These gates were made of wooden slats and were kept locked except for Boat Drill. We walked unmeasured miles every day going to and from the different Pursers' Offices with queries, passports, documents, reports. A special key was issued but if we forgot it the gates could be opened with a coin.

One day I found myself at the gates between First and Cabin Class clutching a bunch of documents. I had forgotten the key and I had no coin in my pocket. I couldn't get through.

'Cooee!' I tried to attract the attention of a Steward or Stewardess. But there was not a soul to be seen on this eighty-three thousand ton ship.

Now in Cunard you don't 'Coeee' anybody but I was getting desperate. They were waiting for these papers in top office. I studied the gate and came to the conclusion there was only one way to get to the other side. Crawl under it. It was forbidden. Conduct unbecoming and all that... I pushed my papers to the other side of the gate and went down on my hands and knees. The floor was filthy. My black tights now had grey knees and my skirt was smeared with dust. Brushing myself down on the other side of the gate I heard heavy footsteps. It was the Master at Arms. I scooped up the papers and hurried to the office. Don't get caught.

Today no one has time to scramble anywhere, the scuppers are disguised, the ships look like hotels and the segregation gates between First, Cabin and Tourist Class are gone for ever.

With this reefer and skirt we wore white shirts and separate Van

Heusen collars. I think perhaps these razor sharp collars will have gone as well. The trick was to anchor this stiff white collar to the shirt with two small studs. One went through a hole in the shirt at the nape of the neck and the other fastened the collar to the shirt where my Adam's apple would have been had I been a man.

One morning I was late up, frantically pulling on clothes and had got to the collar and tie bit when I dropped the collar stud. There I was scrambling around on all fours in a rolling ship. It was nowhere to be seen. I was going to be late. I was going to be in trouble. The Purser would be hungover and he'd give me hell. I used a paper clip and a shipmate came to the rescue with a spare. Solution: carry plenty of studs. I was never caught short again and still have a little box of collar studs. Collector's items now!

Laundering these collars was remarkably easy. We used to wash them at night and plaster them flat on to the mirror over the wash basin. Next morning we peeled them off and they were ready to wear.

Then we had to tie a black tie. Later I was to find the clip-on version in New York. No knots, just a tie already knotted on a clever little plastic clip. One of the Pursers, Ken Allen, had a habit of giving the tie a yank to see if it came off in his hand. It usually did! But I was correctly dressed – even with a clip-on tie. Plain black court shoes with two-inch heel and black nylons for winter completed the image of a Lady Assistant Purser who could have been a *WRNS* Officer or a Prison Officer! But we looked smart and sharp and efficient.

The naval black was worn during the winter months. For the tropics we needed at least six white cotton dresses, available from Harrods, free laundry on board thank goodness. We anchored four Cunard buttons with metal shanks to the front bodice. Tapes secured epaulettes, for distinguishing rank and Department, through eyelets on the shoulders. Plain white court shoes with two-inch heel and we were ready for cruising.

And don't forget the HAT! It was a black tricorn with white crown and a most impressive badge with the Cunard insignia woven in gold thread on red velvet – a lion wearing a crown holding the world in its front paws. The hat was worn for Boat Drills, Burials at Sea and on Captain's instructions.

During one of the interviews I was told that this career post was only available to single women and should I marry my position with the Company would be terminated. Vacancies were few and far between and usually came when a girl left but that didn't happen very often! Millionaires couldn't lure me away from this life on the high seas.

At last my name came to the top of the list. Report to Southampton...

I found my way to the offices in Canute Road where I was fingerprinted, photographed, questioned and given a cup of tea! Then a Seaman's Discharge Book was handed to me. It has a hard cover, blue-green in colour, embossed with gold lettering, much like our original British passports. Every seafarer needs one. The Captain has one, so does the bellboy. This book records the name of every ship in which I sailed, the date and place of engagement and discharge and a report on my ability and general conduct. I was now an Officer in the British Merchant Navy.

I have a vivid recollection of standing like an orphan on the quayside at the Ocean Terminal in Southampton, far from my native Lincolnshire, and just staring up... and up... and up at the two huge red and black funnels of the RMS *Queen Elizabeth*, 83,673 tons, flagship of the fleet. She was gigantic. How did she ever move?

I was checked at the gangway by the Master at Arms, that's the ship's policeman, and presented myself at the First Class Purser's Office as instructed. It was full of Naval Officers, male and female, and it all seemed a bit chaotic. Most of them eyed the new girl with mild curiosity and carried on with their work.

However, a sympathetic Assistant Purser, Eilidh Stewart, a petite and pretty blonde with a dazzling smile, rescued me and took me to a two-berth cabin on B Deck (B.164). I'm sure we walked a mile to get there. It wasn't a very big cabin for two people. It had a porthole, upper and lower bunk beds, two narrow wardrobes, a wash basin and toilet. I would be sharing this cabin with her for the trip, the first of many cabin mates.

She gave me a key to the cabin and told me to always lock the door in port and then she handed me the key to the segregation gates which, as you know, I forgot on my first outing!

I shall always be grateful to Eilidh for integrating me into this new, invigorating world. She did this with a smile, lots of patience, lots of encouragement and wholesome goodwill. We meet at the Cunard Reunions from time to time and I can tell you that she still has all these attributes.

So... I looked, listened, learned and soon lost and found my way around this floating city with its interminable corridors and alleyways. The Verandah Grill, the Observation Lounge, Main Lounge, Smokeroom, Garden Lounge. There were shops, hairdressing salons, cinemas, swimming pools, staterooms and cabins. After all those months of waiting, all the excitement and all the parties, I was on board and about to sail for New York in the largest liner in the world. (1960)

With those interviews and that stenography test engraved on my heart for ever, I was surprised to spend my first day writing names on landing cards. A child could have done it! But that was one of the paradoxical things about the job. It was a mixture of the most mundane tasks like writing landing cards and sorting mail – hundreds and hundreds of letters and telegrams arrived each voyage – to preparing the passenger manifests for the port of arrival. Very important documents which had to be typed, checked and certified as true and correct by the Captain.

Accuracy was of vital importance. There was a fine of $1000 for every typographical error on the United States manifests presented to Immigration Officials on arrival at New York. This was one of the many startling facts I learnt during that first voyage in the Purser's Office on board *Queen Elizabeth*. So get it right!

There was no training period and new girls were thrown in at the deep end. Management considered that with top secretarial experience, having passed all their tests and with a good supply of common sense, they should be able to cope with whatever situation arose.

Fair enough, but I'd never worked in a ship before and there was a new language to learn. Port (left hand side of the ship) and starboard (right hand side of the ship), forward and aft, athwartship corridors (leading from one side of the ship to the other). The floor is the deck; the ceiling is the deckhead. Walls are bulkheads.

Outside the Purser's Office is a large black notice board on a polished wooden plinth. I browsed amongst these notices. Church Services, mail to be collected, competition winners, arrival details, Customs details. A good-looking Purser came to my side and pointed at a bright orange notice (church service) and said,

'Take that down. It's out of date. Throw it in the rosy.'

The rosy? I took it into the office. What's a rosy? It's a waste paper bin, stupid!

It was bedlam at the Purser's Office on that first day of sailing. Passengers bombarded us with questions, forms and tickets and pieces of paper everywhere and I was hot and uncomfortable in collar and tie.

'Where's the Library?'

'What time is it in Mexico City?'

'What time does the sun set today?'

'It's too hot in my cabin.'

'My baggage is missing.'

'I've lost my passport.'

'There's a cockroach in my bathroom.'

But I soon learnt that this was the norm and the tempo settled to a rhythm of Sailing Days, Arrival Days and days at sea in between.

We made our way across the Channel to Cherbourg to repeat the procedure with a French accent. But for the almost imperceptible throb of the engines under my feet I would not have known that we'd sailed.

We heaved and tossed our way across the North Atlantic in all weathers with the tinkling piano of the Palm Court Orchestra in the Main Lounge for afternoon tea and the latest songs of the Beatles pulsating throughout the ship at night. Cunard's gracious style and service ensured that the liners were full to capacity. The Company's slogan was 'Getting there is half the fun' and passengers were offered every conceivable type of food and entertainment during the five-day crossing.

What I did not fully appreciate in those early days of sea-going was that I had also been given some optional extras – adventure, travel, sightseeing and the chance to explore remote parts of the world. I was being paid to do it *and* wear all those diamonds!

So what's it all about then?

There were eight passenger liners in the Cunard fleet when I joined but we had no say as to which ship we were appointed. This was decided by Southampton Office, and we received our instructions to sign off and transfer to another ship by a memo in a little pale green envelope brought on board on arrival in port. We grew to love and hate these little pale green envelopes.

Nor did we have any say about accommodation or who we would be sharing with, and that is why you will hear many different names of cabin mates – Eilidh, Pam, Val, Maureen, Judy, Jane, Julia and many others – it was never a problem for me to share with any of them. These two-berth cabins were scattered all over the ship. Forward at the back of the shops on Prom. Deck, B Deck aft, A Deck, R Deck. Only the two Senior Lady Pursers had their own twin-bedded cabins, en suite.

The *Queen Elizabeth* and *Queen Mary* maintained a weekly service from Southampton to New York and we passed in the middle of the Atlantic Ocean, fifteen miles apart. A wonderful sight on a clear, sunny day.

Top left
WRNS Officer or Prison Officer
(courtesy Ocean Pictures) *Queen Mary.*

Top right
On deck *Queen Elizabeth.*

Bottom left
In tropical whites – ready for
cruising on a windy day *Mauretania*

The *Queen Elizabeth* was the flagship of the fleet and had a Commodore. All other ships had Captains. Both *Queens* carried three classes of passengers. The First Class staterooms were amidships, the most stable in rough weather; Cabin Class was aft and Tourist was forward. In all, just over two thousand passengers (QE 2,260; QM 2,038) and just over one thousand crew (QE 1,296; QM 1,285).

Each Class had its own Purser's Office and Travel Bureau. There were eight Lady Pursers in each *Queen* liner, two of whom were Seniors, one permanently in First Class Purser's Office, one permanently in First Class Travel Bureau. These Seniors blazed the trail for our career afloat. They had been *WRNS* or Army Officers and approached Cunard for a sea-going position. Thanks to them, the Lady Assistant Purser was created.

There was a tendency to call the female Pursers 'Purserettes' but Cunard would have none of it. We were signed on Ship's Articles as Lady Assistant Pursers – A/P (L). Lady Pursers could never be promoted to Purser and it wasn't until the arrival of *Queen Elizabeth 2* that one of my contemporaries, Frances Milroy, achieved that position sailing as Purser. Times change. Congratulations Frances. You made history.

Although the hours were unpredictably long we were given generous leave allowance, usually one trip off every five trips, that's two weeks off every ten weeks. Sometimes we were signed off on 'unattached leave' which usually meant a holiday to use up leave allowance. There were no weekends and there was no such thing as that Monday morning feeling.

Staff was rotated each voyage so that we gained experience in First, Cabin and Tourist Class. We took our meals in the Cabin Class Restaurant in the *Queens* and in the First Class Restaurant in the other ships in the fleet. Smoked salmon, caviar, Beef Wellington, Baked Alaska, Bombe Jubilee, Crêpe Suzettes. And I had never heard of some of the food. For instance, baked okra. No such thing in Lincolnshire!

Hours of duty for ordinary days at sea were nine o'clock until noon then two o'clock until six o'clock with a Rota for what was known as Safe Deposit Duty.

The Safe Deposit, with metal grill doors, was next to the First Class Purser's Office and it stayed open until eight o'clock so that the ladies could choose their jewellery before going to the various cocktail parties around the ship. The boxes contained a mind-boggling treasure of diamonds, rubies, emeralds, gold, silver. Necklaces and bracelets and rings of every description. And they were the real thing – a dazzling experience!

But the most important task after sailing was to muster the passengers, check nationality, passport number and validity, smallpox vaccination and entry visa. Every passenger was asked to complete and sign a Declaration Form. We then had to check and balance these forms against the passenger tickets collected. That is how we arrived at the total number of Adults, Children and Infants on board. Our ACI. This information was sent in coded cable to Southampton or New York depending in which direction we were travelling.

After the muster came the typing of the manifests – two sets – Westbound US Citizens and Aliens. Eastbound we mustered passengers in the same way. One list for passengers disembarking France, the other for the United Kingdom. The UK forms were enormous, about thirty-six inches square, needing a steam-roller of a typewriter. The forms were simple enough to type once tabulated but we got into real difficulties in rough weather. The typewriter carriage just would not move when the ship was rolling. A problem with gravity. A thick rubber band fixed to the roller sometimes helped but one afternoon when we were being chased by Hurricane Cleo we just closed the office. It was impossible to type.

A Crew List had to be prepared and typed each voyage giving name, date and place of birth, rank and position on board. Pages and pages of it, listing every crew member, more than one thousand two hundred names. This, too, was required by the American Immigration Officials.

I was bashing away at this list on my first trip when I came across 'Gardener'. I did a double take. We have a Gardener on board? Signed on Ship's Articles! It was true.

One morning I was making my way through the Main Lounge when I met this quiet, unassuming man roaming the ship with his watering can tending the plants and floral displays. Eric Littaur played an integral role in maintaining Cunard's gracious style of living.

We had some evening duties.

'It's M & M night tonight,' announced the Senior Assistant Purser, 'be there 7p.m.'

I didn't know what it meant so I asked Eilidh when I got back to the cabin. 'What's M & M? Mambo and Maracas, a Latin American party? Masks and Mermaids? Mud and Men?'

'No,' she smiled, 'it's Mixing and Mingling. And can be boring. Don't get stuck. Keep moving.'

All Heads of Departments held cocktail parties every day at sea. The Lady Purser was responsible for getting the lists of guests from Captain, Staff Captain, Purser, Principal Medical Officer, Chief Steward and Chief Engineer. We then had to check that there were no duplications, that the stateroom number was correct and make sure the right guests went to the right Officer. Then we typed the lists of guests for each party. This was an aide-memoire for the host and also a check as to who attended and who did not – and why not? Perhaps they were ill. Check!

But cocktail cards could disappear. I remember one occasion when tempers rose, blood pressure soared and the Captain nearly had a heart attack. This is what happened. It had been decided that passengers were to be invited by their tables in the Restaurant. The cards were prepared, checked and the bell boy took them to the Restaurant for distribution.

At seven o'clock the Captain, Staff Captain, Chief Officer, Chief Engineer, Principal Medical Officer and all the Senior Officers were in their own day rooms, fully decked out in mess kit, preening every once in a while before the mirror and pacing up and down waiting for the guests to arrive. No one appeared. At any party. The phones were red hot.

'What the bloody hell...' The Purser was incandescent.

A big investigation rolled through the Departments. The invitation cards had never been put on the tables. Someone had shoved them into a cupboard in the Restaurant!

The passengers were unaware that they should have been at a cocktail party so we wrote the invitations again for the next evening. Parties were held pre-lunch and pre-dinner when we were at full capacity. That's quite a lot of invitations and this work was in addition to the routine preparation of manifests, answering telephones, stenography appointments and dealing with a constant stream of passengers at the counter.

A Fancy Headdress Parade was held once each trip. Passengers were encouraged to make a hat depicting a song title. We gave each entrant a number and then they were paraded around the dance floor by one of our young Pursers to be judged by a panel of passengers chosen by the Purser.

It was important that we generated interest to ensure a good turnout. By ten o'clock at night the passengers were feeling no pain and some entries came to grief long before they got in front of the judges.

Every voyage we could guarantee 'One Alone' – a bald-headed man with a pipe cleaner curled into a spiral, stuck to his pate with sellotape. A favourite was 'Melancholy Baby' – a masterpiece created from a cauliflower and a melon! Another regular was 'Time on my Hands' – a pair of white gloves, stuffed and taped to the head, cradling an alarm clock which was too heavy and clattered to the deck. It rarely made the circuit.

Both *Queen* liners operated Travel Bureaux in each Class and after we had gained experience in the Pursers' Offices we would be assigned to the Travel Bureau. Here we dealt with air, rail and bus tickets, hotel accommodation, car hire and theatre tickets for New York or London. All booked by cable or radio telephone.

Eastbound we had to see every passenger to find out whether he/she needed a ticket to Paris or London so that we could order the train for each port of disembarkation.

'Good morning, Madam, are you disembarking at Cherbourg or Southampton?'

'Yes, that's right,' was the smiling reply.

We then cabled our Paris and London offices for the appropriate size of train. We were responsible for all business transacted in the Travel Bureau and handled thousands of American dollars, UK sterling and French francs by selling tickets to any destination in the world. We balanced every day at close of business and paid the money to the Purser. All shortfalls – mistakes – had to be made good by the Lady Purser.

The travel requirements of some of our passengers stretched our ingenuity to the limit at times. Whole compartments in trains for sole occupancy; a white Rolls-Royce at the quay-side for a world-famous film star – Elizabeth Taylor; a chartered plane. On one occasion we arranged a complete train for Count Folke and Countess Christine Bernadotte and other members of the Swedish Royal family from Cherbourg to Stockholm, liaising with the Royal Palace in Stockholm for the configuration of carriages.

The voyage from Southampton to New York took five days – weather permitting. During that time hundreds and hundreds of passengers would be seen, documented, fed, entertained and transported.

Behind the scenes pressure built up as we approached land. Voyage Reports from the Captain, Staff Captain, Purser, Chief Engineer, Principal Medical Officer – all had to be typed and signed ready for arrival.

Damaged Clothing Report – soot from the funnels spoiling a dress or jacket, spilt food in the Restaurants, torn dress in the Main Lounge – it was amazing how much clothing got damaged in such a civilised ship.

Orchestra Report – giving the behaviour and performance of the bands playing in each Class.

Film Report – passenger reaction to the films shown during the voyage.

Typewriter Report – to repair bits that had broken or dropped off in bad weather.

Deck Games Requisition – new quoits, table tennis balls, shuffle board sticks.

And don't forget the Pre-embarkation Inspection letter for New York! First trippers found two more fictitious reports to prepare. Rat Report and the Oil Report. How many rats had been sighted and how much green oil to order for the starboard lights! I was detailed to make the Oil Report.

'Take your notebook and go down below, find the Second Engineer and ask how much green oil we need to order for the starboard lights. And get him to sign it.'

Off I went, as daft as a brush. Going down below was scary but interesting. Slippery metal companionways, meshed walkways. Shiny pipes, deafening noise, insufferable heat. Here was another world. These huge, polished chunks of metal churning and clattering and banging while, up above, the passengers sipped their champagne and nibbled at the caviar canapés.

The crew was familiar with these mean tricks and went along with it. But we were all as bad when we were no longer first trippers.

Rumours ran riot in ships and they always started in the Galley, and what is more, they were usually correct! Why? How could the Vegetable Cook know what was happening on both sides of the Atlantic? Listen to this! My steward told me, in all seriousness, that the Spud Machine was responsible.

'You'll never guess what, Miss Arnold?'

I had gone back to the cabin for some papers and the steward was finishing the bathroom.

'There's a longshoremen's strike in New York. It'll bugger up our arrival. And I'm on leave next trip.'

'How do you know?' I asked.

'The Spud (potato) Machine,' he replied. 'In the Galley.'

'Don't believe it,' I paused in the doorway.

'S'right.' The steward flicked a cloth across the mirror. 'It picks up the radio messages to the Radio Room. Ya know, it's several decks above the Galley. That's why the fellows working in the Galley allus get to know what's going on.'

ETA – Estimated Time of Arrival and ETD – Estimated Time of Departure cables were in the Company's five-letter code. The Purser's Office was responsible for coding and decoding these messages. I liked this work. There was always the element of mystery as to what would emerge. It could be anything from 'Serve bottle of champagne to...' or 'Regret to report...' and once a great hush descended upon the office when a Q message came in. The Q decoding book was locked away in the Purser's safe. Someone had to go and ask him for it whatever the time, day or night. This particular message referred to a murder in Southampton during our port stay and it contained instructions about enquiries to be made on board.

These messages had to be decoded by one Assistant Purser and countersigned as correct by another before delivery to the Captain. The five-letter coding was eventually abandoned to plain language except for the top secret Q code messages.

We often arrived New York at dawn. On my first trip I couldn't contain myself. New York! New York! I went to the Boat Deck to get my first glimpse. It was cold and clear with a crystalline glow to the Manhattan skyscrapers as the launch nudged alongside. I watched the Pilot and other officials scramble up the rope ladder dangling on that black cliff face. Then the slow, majestic voyage up river, past the Statue of Liberty. We had arrived – Southampton was an ocean away.

We had grappled with a mountain of exacting paper work, we had checked accounts, we had prepared Voyage Reports and we had struggled to balance the manifests. Sometimes it took hours to find an error, working into the early hours checking and re-checking. The reason was usually someone with dual nationality passports appearing on the US Citizens and Aliens manifest. A duplicated entry. The simplest, most careless mistake but balance we must even if it took all night.

There were many Spanish-speaking passengers on board. Mexicans, Cubans, Costa Ricans, South Americans, Spaniards. And, of course, we were at Cherbourg within hours of leaving Southampton. So in spite of the toil and sweat and agony of it all, those language tests were all important.

We had met charming passengers who would be on our Christmas card list for years to come, we had placated angry passengers who complained about anything from the caviar to the bad weather which was all our fault. We had sympathised with the seasick passengers... we had rubbed shoulders with the rich and the famous at those cocktail parties.

So that was what it was all about... It had been worth it. Shipboard life suits the vagabond in me. Always on the move. All the different people, all the different sights and sounds. It's exciting to feel the engines come to life under my feet and I love to walk on deck on a crystal, clear morning, our wake stretching away to the horizon and the sun tinting the sea until it looks like pinky gold satin. And the sea at night is just as beautiful. At times you can almost reach for a star in that black velvet sky. A diary entry the night after sailing on that first trip reads: 'Magnificent night, stars, slight breeze'. The elements have never ceased to make me wonder.

But there was more... much more to come. There was cruising in the Caribbean, cruising in the Mediterranean... and cruising round the world.

Rules And Regulations

Lots of rules and regulations in Cunard. In fact, there was a book full of them. The Blue Book. On board we were never allowed out of uniform so we were never really off duty. Walking on deck at midnight we could be asked 'What time do we dock?' or 'I think my little boy has measles,' or simply 'I've lost my way.'

Of course, in the cabin we could wear what we wanted but we could be called out at any time – to decode a cable, to comfort a passenger who had just received bad news, to act as interpreter, it could be anything and we had to scramble into uniform before showing our nose outside the cabin. Go...go...go...

Discipline was strict both for officers and ratings. If a waiter put his serving cloth under his arm it was a dismissal offence. I thought of that recently when I read the reports of the food hygiene scare on cruise ships arriving New York.

The Lady Pursers' hair must be worn off the collar. We were not allowed to wear jewellery. No coloured nail polish. No deviation from uniform regulations. One Lady Purser who had come from another shipping company insisted on wearing a black belt with her white uniform dress. Not allowed! No eating at the counter. No walking about the ship with reefer unfastened. No running along the corridors. No entertaining members of the opposite sex in our cabins after 8p.m....

Rules are made to be broken and we sailed close to the wind. We had lots of parties in our cabins. We knew that if we were caught we would be for the high jump but we managed to get away with it and had some glorious wing-dingers. We had plenty of booze. Each trip we were issued with Officer's Low Rate allowance. A bottle of Scotch cost sixteen shillings (80p), gin twelve shillings (60p), sherry twelve shillings (60p).

On closing the office, all typewriters had to be put on the deck and all desk tops cleared in case bad weather blew up during the night. This habit was hard to kick when I came ashore. My colleagues couldn't understand my neurotic clearing of the desks every night.

Bridge Orders were issued by the Captain and his Officers on Watch. These were written in a Bridge Order Book and a Bridge Messenger visited every Department in the ship to get a signature confirming receipt of the message. Each Department was then responsible for carrying out the Order.

When we got into bad weather the Bridge Orders came thick and fast. Close portholes, deadlight portholes (a deadlight is a metal disc fitted over the porthole so that the sea cannot break the glass), rig rolling lines – thick, velvety ropes across the open spaces so that passenger could grab them if the ship lurched. Open decks were out of bounds and with all doors and portholes closed the ship got hot and smelly. Many passengers were seasick especially in Tourist Class. They were at the sharp end and took every pitch and roll personally.

The North Atlantic run was tough during the winter months and we were often in terrible weather. Sometimes we got bad weather during the summer, too. The roughest storm I've ever known was mid-August, mid-Atlantic. We were at the height of the summer season sailings and the ship was bursting at the seams with not a berth to spare. Eighty thousand tons of metal creaked and groaned and rattled and shuddered and sighed as we ploughed our way through a tumultuous mountain of raging hills and valleys of frothing foam and screaming winds. We had to reduce speed which meant that we were late arriving in port causing delays and disruption to passengers' onward travel.

Diary note, *Queen Mary* 1965: '196 passengers invited to midday Cocktail Party but only 37 came. Evening parties a failure, too'.

During one voyage in September two portholes in a First Class cabin were smashed by the sea. An elderly couple were in bed and suffered minor cuts to their faces. The beds were saturated with sea water. First Class accommodation is high above the water line so you'll realise just how powerful those waves had been.

Keys! Guard them with your life. The Staff Purser (Accounts) was responsible for all cash transactions throughout the ship. He slept with his keys under his pillow. At the beginning of each voyage he issued large sums of dollars and sterling as floats. We signed for them and had to make good any losses. One night, at a party, I lost my bunch of keys and spent many anxious hours searching. Luckily for me, a Stewardess found them but I had to make a report to the Staff

Captain. Where was I? Chatting with friends. Fib. A fate worse than death awaits anyone careless with keys.

I once saw a Purser deliberately lift a bunch of keys lying on top of a desk in the office. He sat back and waited for the hullabaloo to die down. Then he returned the keys to the person concerned and delivered his reprimand in due Purser fashion! I quickly learned to be extremely key-conscious.

We were not allowed to dance with passengers and I didn't feel at all deprived since bouncing around the Main Lounge in a collar and tie was not my idea of fun. But on the smaller ships protocol was a little more relaxed and the Purser would often encourage us to join in. We were not allowed to change but after a drink or two we didn't notice or care that we were 'cutting a rug' in a black uniform with collar and tie!

Cruising was a different matter. There was a tremendous carnival atmosphere and everyone was having a wonderful time and we longed to join in. I accepted a dare on the *Mauretania* which nearly cost me my job. I'll tell you about it later.

Homeward bound we suffered from something called 'The Channels' – the excitement and anticipation of coming back to the home port. This malady was exacerbated by Obligato Night – the night before docking – when we had to consume drink that was over and above our Customs allowance. Any contravention of Customs regulations was a serious matter leading to dismissal. But drink can be disguised.

A tumbler of white rum with a toothbrush in it sounds a bit desperate but I've known colleagues get away with it. The water flask can also be filled but it's too risky. Rummagers (Customs Officers) come on board to give us the once-over and they know where to look. So the drink had to be drunk or poured down the loo. It was crazy, it was fun, it was Obligato Night. I found the best cure for a hangover was French onion soup. It was always on the breakfast menu in those days!

Often a passenger would leave a bottle of champagne at the Purser's Office during disembarking. Obligato Night had come and gone and there we were with illicit hooch. We drank it out of tea cups – a bit of an insult to the champagne but it went down well after a 6a.m. call for duty!

An American passenger gave me her gorgeous floral arrangement in a ceramic pot before she left the ship in Southampton. The Rummagers swooped on us, sifting through the soil and then plonked the savaged plant back in the pot. They found nothing.

Then the gangway was in place and the ship swarmed with management and visitors and for us there was the excitement of the pale green envelopes, personal mail, getting off duty, shopping and a long, glorious sleep.

Take A Letter Miss ...

The reason for that high speed technical, brutal shorthand paper testing us about the globules of water on the ship's propeller became clear to me once I got to sea. Cunard advertised their shipboard stenography service in a leaflet readily available to passengers. It set out the charges for stenography, copy-typing and dictaphone work. We didn't know what the dictation was about until we got to the appointment. It could be anything from milking machines to china clay to nuclear science, to psychoanalysis. Be prepared.

But a flurry of steno. appointments really stretched us to the limit. They were in addition to the preparation of manifests, cocktail invitations, voyage reports and the endless stream of passengers at the counter. All work had to be completed before arrival. To keep abreast of the workload we would often go back to the office after dinner and just crack on, often into the early hours, with the Night Steward keeping us going with a tray of hot coffee and sandwiches. What would we have done without them?

I enjoyed the steno. appointments. We could be working for Counts, Diplomats, film stars, business men, authors. Fascinating stuff.

My first appointment came the day after sailing from Cherbourg and left me no time for nerves. A famous French Count, Le Comte de Chambrun, had some important dictation. He was a direct descendant of the Marquis de La Fayette who had excelled himself during the American War of Independence and was travelling to the mid-West to open a new building to commemorate the name of his forebear.

The dictation, the speech he was to deliver, was in perfect English and I had no problems apart from physical ones. I found the shirt cuffs and thick uniform an awful nuisance for speedy writing and my starched collar was so uncomfortable. By the end of the day my neck was red raw!

I had never even written the word 'nuclear' in shorthand until I was booked for an appointment with an Atomic Scientist. The work was so top secret that I was allocated a stateroom on 'A' Deck and locked in! When I'd finished the work he came to collect it and asked me to hand over every piece of paper, clean and spoiled, including the used carbon papers.

There was often the thrill of working for a film star wanting to write 'thank you' letters. A great talking point when we got back to our cabin in the evening to swap notes about what they were really like, what they were wearing, what they had on their dressing table – what brand of make-up they used and which perfume they wore!

I had a stenography appointment with Dr Erich Fromm, a psychoanalyst and outstanding social scientist and author. His books had always interested me and to sit there, opposite him, breathing the same air, actually working for him really was something. I remember him as a bespectacled, dapper little man with a shock of white hair. The first letter he dictated was to Dr Albert Schweitzer's Assistant in Lambaréné followed by another one to Bertrand Russell in Wales. He also dictated some chapters for his latest book on Socialist Humanism.

On another occasion I sat poised opposite a Canadian diplomat and he began:

'This first letter is to the Prime Minister of Canada. Dear Lester...' (The Rt. Hon. Lester B. Pearson).

Lady Chatterjee, a charming English lady, (née Gladys Broughton) was a Barrister at Lincoln's Inn, widow of Sir Atul Chandra Chatterjee, formerly High Commissioner for India and adviser to Secretary of State for India. She gave me a lot of dictation on Juvenile Deliquency.

Baroness von Gottenburg dictated a lengthy paper on German Re-unification – on board *Queen Elizabeth* 1963. It took a little time didn't it?

I also worked for the South African Minister of Commerce but I don't have a note of his name.

There was no special office for stenography appointments. The passenger could choose his or her stateroom or a corner of the Writing Room, the Main Lounge or the Library.

I only had one unpleasant experience. A passenger booked an appointment and I went along to his stateroom at the designated time. He was a man of fifty something, swarthy complexion, balding, plump, wearing spectacles. To my amazement he was in bed with papers and files strewn around him! I thought I must have made a mistake with the time of the appointment.

'Oh, I'm sorry. Perhaps you will ring the Purser's Office when you are ready.'

'No... No... No. I'm ready. Please sit down.' And he points to the chair at the side of his bed.

I do. But my antenna is finely tuned. This is a bizarre situation. After dictating for half an hour or so he stops. I look up. He has pushed his papers – and the bedclothes – away from him. I scoop up my notebook and move towards the door. 'I'll let you have the work as soon as it is ready,' and left quickly.

Some hours later I sent the work to him in a folder with the Cunard account. He telephoned the office and asked me to go to his stateroom.

I grabbed my notebook again and arrived at his stateroom. He was sitting at the writing desk.

'I want to pay you personally for the work.' He doesn't look at me.

'But...but... I am employed by Cunard and the account must be settled at the Purser's Office. You will be issued with an official receipt.'

'But I want to pay you...'

I wasn't going to get into an argument and reiterated that the account should be paid at the Purser's Office and an official receipt given.

This was an alarming development so when I got back to the office I told the Purser the whole story. He asked me to make a report. Good job I did. The passenger complained that my work was unsatisfactory and refused to pay the bill! Today, the phrase 'sexual harassment' springs to mind!

But there were many very interesting stenography appointments and they often led to offers of employment. A delegation from the Association of American Railroads was travelling westbound. They had spent months in Russia looking at their systems, riding the length and breadth of their railroads and they wanted to prepare reports during the voyage. This was a massive undertaking and several of us were taken off Purser duty to do this important work.

My diary reads: 'Beginning to feel the strain but how satisfying to know that I can still be a good secretary. The bill came to $253.00 – must be an all time record'. A lot of midnight oil was burnt during this voyage. The Head of the Delegation, Mr C. D. Buford, the Vice President, offered me a job in Washington and followed it up with a letter and contract but... the call of the sea was too strong!

We carried large numbers of Masons, Rotarians, Lions and Kiwanis and they always held meetings on board. Special attendance cards were printed and signed by the Purser and we had all the paraphernalia required for each group. After the meetings we prepared the Minutes. They were signed by the Purser and circulated.

On reflection, I wonder how we ever got through such a mountain of work. This was long before the days of word processors but we did, and the high tech. world we enjoy today was undreamed of as we rolled across the Atlantic in a Force 8 gale bashing away on our manual typewriters with thirty-inch carriages! Fiddling with carbon papers. No over-types, amendments or errors were allowed. And we had no boob juice (Tippex Corrector Fluid) or photo-copy machines. Eight copies of the manifest were needed for New York. If you made a mistake when carboning up and didn't make enough copies you had to type the document all over again. Oh! Happy Days!

Arrivals and Departures

The best laid schemes of mice and men came to naught if there was a birth or death on board. The manifests were no longer accurate and had to be re-typed to give correct number of souls on board. Once again, the Captain would sign the manifests 'Certified as true and correct...' before arrival.

The memory of a personally shocking incident on the *Ivernia* stays with me still. The *Ivy* maintained the UK to Canada service along with three sister ships. A Mrs Craig, first class passenger, had not presented herself at the Purser's Office and we needed the information so that we could complete the manifests. I went to see her. I found a small, slim lady with short, dark hair beginning to grey, deep brown eyes and sallow complexion. Let's say mid- to late forties.

'Good afternoon, Mrs Craig, it's just routine. We need to complete the manifests for arrival. May I see your passport please?' (She was 49).

As I checked the details her thin, twiggy fingers were fidgeting with the clasp of her black leather handbag.

'I'm visiting my son,' she said. 'He's to be married. Soon.' She fixed me with her disappointed eyes. 'I'm not happy about it.'

'Oh! I'm sure everything will turn out well.' I decided not to pursue the problem. 'Thank you, Mrs Craig. Landing cards will be issued tomorrow.' I handed back the passport. 'They'll be serving tea in the Lounge. Why don't you go along and join them,' I suggested and left.

The next morning, the Stewardess, Maria Pons, found Mrs Craig dead in bed. We were still in the Atlantic and had been through some rough weather during the night. Mrs Craig's handbag had fallen from a small shelf above her bed and was covering her face. Cables, cables, and more cables coded to Quebec and Southampton. I was called to the Captain's dayroom to take verbatim notes from Maria, the Spanish Stewardess. My diary reads: 'Maria's accent was a bit tricky but I got it all back and the Captain was satisfied.'

We were held in the St Lawrence River until the Coroner came on board. Then the yellow quarantine flag was hoisted. The ship had not been cleared for entry to port. Now the passengers were getting angry but we were powerless to move until the officials were satisfied about cause of death. The ship was cleared for docking late afternoon but many onward travel arrangements had to be rearranged. And we were in the Canadian news.

At sea anything can and did happen. I suppose this is one of the attractions. Never a dull moment. The *Mauretania* was approaching New York and it was the night before arrival. I was in the restaurant having dinner when the Doctor sent a message for me to go to a Tourist Class cabin immediately.

A young Peruvian woman, nineteen years old, was in labour with her first child. This slip of a girl, with her huge, glistening eyes and curtain of black hair lay perspiring in the lower bunk bed whilst her husband paced the hot and stuffy little cabin, beside himself with anxiety. I, too, was full of apprehension. My Spanish studies had not included childbirth phraseology so there was much frenetic thumbing through the dictionary to get the answers to the questions the Doctor was asking.

The young woman was transferred to the hospital. It is one deck below the passenger decks, spotless and white, all clinically orderly and correct, looking much the same as hospitals ashore, the only difference being that equipment, beds and anything that can move, is anchored with shiny, chrome attachments to bulkhead or deck.

I was warned that I may be needed during the night. I wasn't, and the lovely young Peruvian was transferred to hospital to give birth to her baby in New York the next morning. So the manifests remained 'Certified as true...'

One afternoon, mid-Atlantic, on board *Queen Elizabeth*, eastbound, the Table Tennis Tournament was in full swing. The sea was as calm as a mill pond, the sun was shining and everyone was having a wonderful time. Suddenly one of the players, a good-looking, dark-haired man, forty-something, as lean and muscular as they come, slumped across the table. The Doctor and Nursing Sister were summoned immediately and he was transferred to hospital but he was dead.

It was the task of the Lady Purser to help the bereaved passenger. We needed information about relatives, arrangements for disembarkation, onward travel and most difficult of all, their wishes about the disposal of remains. It is very harrowing (and expensive) dealing with a dead body in foreign ports.

The Landing Agent had to be notified and he had to contact Immigration, Customs, Port Health Authorities for clearance who then have to contact hospital, doctor and Undertakers. And a Death Certificate was needed before anything can happen. Everyone charges fees. They vary from country to country.

Then there was the emotional anguish of waiting for replies to cables and phone calls through the different time zones. I was always amazed how calm the bereaved were when coping with it all in an enormous liner, in a vast ocean, so far from familiar surroundings. It was such a devastating blow to them but somehow they maintained a great peace and dignity through it all.

The most difficult death I remember occurred on the *Mauretania* Mediterranean Cruise 1962. We were arriving Port Said, Egypt early in the morning. I remember her as a gracious sixty year old who enjoyed playing Bridge. She suffered a cerebral haemorrhage and died at 8.50 a.m. Cables were coded for Liverpool, London and New York but the Egyptians refused to accept coded messages so we had to start all over again.

Meanwhile the authorities refused to clear the ship. No one was allowed down the gangway. The lady could have been murdered! Eventually they satisfied themselves about the cause of death and demanded that the body be embalmed or buried within twenty-four hours! They had to be dissuaded. It took a little time but our Doctor won the day. No embalming.

This lady was travelling alone and we had to trace next of kin. After trawling through the manifests for information, I was escorted down the gangway by an Egyptian policeman to the Agent's office. Eventually I spoke to her nephew in Dorset. Clearance then had to be given for the body to be removed from the ship, lists of her effects had to be made by a Purser in company with the Master at Arms, then the inventory had to be typed, signed and witnessed. Manifests to alter. Safe Deposit to clear. Endless paperwork and officialdom. The toing and froing with officials, Port Health authorities and Immigration officers went on most of the day.

Meanwhile, on the dockside, more than a dozen luxury coaches were sizzling in the heat waiting to take passengers on tour to Cairo, Luxor and the Aswan Dam. On board seven hundred passengers were baying for our blood.

In September 1965 the *Franconia* (formerly *Ivernia*) deserted Canada and joined the cruise scene. We sailed from Southampton for a Mediterranean cruise. A middle-aged man, travelling alone, died the night we docked at Funchal, Madeira. I was on the Duty Rota and after many cables and telephone calls to trace next of kin it was requested that the passenger be buried at an English church in Funchal.

Both *Queen* liners operated Travel Bureaux.
First class Travel Bureau *Queen Mary*
(courtesy Ocean Pictures)

Cabin Class Travel Bureau *Queen Elizabeth*
(courtesy Ocean Pictures)

With the help of the Company's Agents it was all arranged. A car was provided for the Cruise Director, Harold Grimes, and me to follow the hearse to a deserted, windswept hillside and we stood by the grave to pay our first and last respects on behalf of all who knew him. I had never set eyes on the man. A strange experience.

The *Mauretania*, en route to New York. We were chasing up a Tourist passenger who hadn't presented himself at the office for documentation check. He was found dead in his cabin. A fifty-four year old man in possession of an American passport, a Canadian passport and a British passport – sort that one out.

All these problems have to be solved quickly. No good leaving anything until tomorrow. We are moving all the time and we have a schedule to maintain. Here's an interesting entry in my diary *Mauretania*, eastbound. 'Wednesday, 25th July 1962. Tourist Class passenger died during the night. Friday, 27th July. Arrived Cobh, Eire, 7a.m. Extremely busy with additional documents for body of Tourist passenger to be landed here. Sailed 10a.m.' Three hours alongside!

These days I like to travel alone in cargo ships to the west coast of South America and the first thing I do when I get on board is to give the Captain details of my next of kin, disposal instructions and a copy of my travel and medical insurance. I wouldn't inflict that work upon anyone!

And then there was an attempted suicide. We were mid-Atlantic travelling eastbound, *Mauretania*. I put my coat over my uniform to walk on deck after dinner. The deck was deserted but for two ladies, one older than the other, mother and daughter perhaps. I passed by, strolled to the end of the deck, turned and came back. They were having a heated argument in Spanish. As I got nearer the older of the two women ran to the boat rail, paused, then threw one leg over the rail. She meant business. I ran to grab her and the other woman did the same and together we pulled her back on to the deck. We got her down below to her cabin with loud wailing and protestation.

They were Mexicans. Aunt and niece, and the aunt wanted to end it all. She said she never wanted to make the voyage in the first place. She was quite hysterical so I telephoned the hospital and a Nursing Sister came and took care of things. I then reported the incident to the Bridge and the Purser.

In Tourist Class, *Queen Elizabeth*, eastbound, a Miss Rosalind Smith, travelling alone, was causing quite a stir among the young Pursers. She was having a wonderful time dancing in the Lounge and partying until the early hours.

In the Tourist Purser's Office, everyone was plodding on with their paperwork when one of the young Pursers said,

'Ros didn't stay in the Lounge very long last night.' He was speaking to no one in particular. 'Said she wasn't feeling very well.'

'No,' the Tourist Purser piped up. He was in The Box, an office in the corner that was his, and his alone. There was only room for a small desk, a chair and a huge safe. 'And you won't be seeing her there again.'

'Why not?' asked the young admirer. 'What's happened?'

'She gave birth to a baby boy at four o'clock this morning. Four and a half pounds. And,' the Purser came out of his Box and locked the door, 'she's asked for the baby to be registered in another name.' He lit a cigarette. 'No chance. Make sure the manifest is amended and ready for signature by the Captain again.' And off he went for his heart-starter.

I only attended one passenger burial at sea. The *Queen Elizabeth 2* had just left Kota Kinabalu, Sabah (formerly North Borneo) and we were sailing the South China Sea. A retired couple were making their first World Cruise and doing what they had come to do. Enjoy themselves. I remember this man well. He was as chirpy as a cricket, lean, energetic, joining in everything and dancing the night away with his wife. He collapsed in the Double Down Room and died a few hours later.

We put all the alternatives to his widow. Burial at the next port, burial at sea, disembarkation and flying home with the deceased. She decided on burial at sea. The service was conducted by the Captain on the After Deck at 7 o'clock in the morning. The speed was reduced so that the ship was almost stationary in the water. I was amazed that the South China Sea was such a sludgy, muddy colour.

And crew members died on board. It came as a big shock to the ship's company when it happened. Often it was their wish for burial at sea.

Bob Agnew, Barman, had been at sea for years and his father before him had been a Cunarder. This cheery, lovable rogue was ideally suited to the job. A big softie with rosy cheeks tingeing to mauve, straggly damp hair – he perspired a lot – and he had a smile for everyone.

I'd just finished organising the Bridge Tournament in the Smoke Room and was on my way back to the office. He was behind his Bar, tinkering with the glasses.

'How's things? Good trip?' I asked, meaning plenty of tips from the passengers.

'Not bad but no sweat. Ya, see, Miss. It's easy. Dead easy.' He sniffed and yanked on his waistcoat. It was too tight. 'Ya don't have to worry about dropsy (tips). All you do is you puts a quarter, you know, a twenty-five cent piece, in the bottom of the tot measure and you just pours in the whisky or gin. Nobody knows its there, ya see. And we've soon got a spare bottle on our hands. Me and me mate. We splits it.'

'You mean, you can save all that just by putting a coin in the measure?'

'S'right Miss. Displacement. Now, not a word. Got time for a quickie?'

'No, sorry. Must get back.' I was surprised he told me about this fraud, scam, trick – call it what you will. Even barmen need someone to talk to now and again.

One morning, mid-Atlantic, the Steward couldn't wake him up. Bob had slipped his leash.

Before the burial we raided the flower vases placed outside the staterooms at night, taking a bloom here and a bloom there – no one would miss one – so that there were flowers on the coffin which wasn't a coffin. The body is stitched into tarpaulin by the Bo'sun and placed on a trestle near the open boat rail on the After Deck. It looks like a black log draped with the Union flag. At a given point in the Service, the trestle is raised at one end and the 'log' slips into the sea. For me there is something quite appeasing to watch the flowers drifting in the wake of the ship bringing a splash of colour to that vast expanse of ocean, all calm and quiet.

And ships departed from our lives. I recall with deep sorrow the day I watched the *Mauretania* sail down Southampton Water with that long paying-off pennant, trailing in the breeze. It was twenty-six yards long, denoting a yard for every year of service. It was 10 November 1965. She was going to the breaker's yard. It was unbearable. Such a wonderful ship, such a wonderful crew, such wonderful passengers. Images that never fade and the memories are mine.

In 1967 the *Queen Mary* departed these shores but she lives on at Long Beach, California. My diary (31 October) says: 'I went to the Photo-copy room on the third floor at 9.30 a.m. to wait for the *Mary* to go by. There was a fly past of helicopters in the shape of an anchor, aeroplanes, tugs, fire tenders – everything that could float accompanied her down Southampton Water – Vaya con Dios – and the rest of the day was sad for me'.

The Professional Virgins

So what did we do after the office closed? We couldn't catch a No. 9 bus and go home but as Officers we did enjoy some passenger amenities. We were allowed to go to the Cinema showing different films each evening, usually the latest releases. We could use the

Gymnasium, Swimming Pool and Squash Court. We played liar dice, chess, dominoes, read books, wrote, painted, knitted and sewed, etcetera, and we were invited to the Officers' Wardroom.

When we got alongside there was a Port Duty Rota showing who was on duty and for how long. In New York a gang of us would go ice skating at Rockefeller Plaza. It was exhilarating after being cooped up on 83,000 tons of floating metal.

There were always interesting shows on Broadway. We couldn't book in advance but we were often able to get tickets at the Box Office on the night of the performance. And if the star of the show had travelled with us we could get lucky. Harry Belafonte invited Pam and me backstage at his theatre.

Broadway was wonderful at night in the rain with its psychedelic lights weeping and blinking and car tyres peeling coloured strips from the road.

We got some unusual perks in the Travel Bureau. Representatives from the hotels we booked would meet the ship on arrival New York. One of the most prized was to be offered a complimentary room in one of their hotels. It was such bliss to get away from the ship and eat different food and sleep in a proper bed that didn't move. Our bunk beds were comfortable but narrow. I'm not very tall but it was easy to get bruised knees and elbows in rough weather. Upper berth was best because I could sit up in bed. Impossible in the lower berth.

So after all passengers had disembarked, all books had been balanced and all paper work was ready for sailing again we would change, pack an overnight bag and check in to our free hotel room. I remember Hotel Wentworth and Hotel Governor Clinton and on one voyage Maureen and I were invited to a luxury hotel in Atlantic City. It was against the rules to sleep off the ship. Just don't get caught!

We did an enormous amount of business with the airlines. One of my first bookings was for two seats on a flight to Anchorage, Alaska! The airline representatives expressed their appreciation in many different ways. I will describe one of the most unique I enjoyed. Listen to this.

Four of us are sitting side by side in the back seat of a police patrol car. Ahead of us a mile of grey concrete stretches to infinity. It's a runway.

'Is that where we're going?' Ann asks, 'I can't look.' All around planes are landing and climbing into the sky.

'It's OK.' The policeman turns to look at us, flicking his peaked hat with his thumb, setting it at a non-regulation angle. 'Don't worry.'

It is 14 March 1961. The *Queen Elizabeth* had docked early. Four of us in the Travel Bureau – Barbara, Ann, Paula and I have been invited by Trans-World Airlines to visit Idlewild (now J. F. Kennedy) airport. Our hostess arranged for a chauffeur-driven Cadillac to collect us from the ship. At the airport we transfer to a police patrol car to take us all over the airfield.

'This'll be the thrill of the day, trust me,' the policeman flashes his perfect white teeth at us. We can hear the crackle of voices on his car radio picking up instructions from the Control Tower to the planes coming in to land. 'Get ready now, relax,' he revs his engine. 'Here we go.'

I can see his eyes narrowing in the driving mirror, his jaw is set rigid. About a hundred yards away, on a parallel runway to our right, a huge jet is roaring in anger, restless for take-off. Now it's gathering speed, the rage of its engines deafening us. The race is on. We are scorching along and there are still miles of runway ahead but the airliner is already smelling freedom. It's up and away. Our car slows down and we gaze at the sliver of silver until it is lost in the clouds.

We are then driven to the Control Tower with rows and rows of men sitting at large screens and playing horizontal piano keys – or so it seems. From that height the panoramic view of the airfield is wider and deeper than anyone can imagine. Once again we hear instructions being given to the pilots. It's all so intense, so concentrated, so dangerous!

The policeman was right. It had been a thrilling day and I'm quite sure that no Lady Pursers are invited to JFK today and certainly do not race jet airliners along runways in a police patrol car!

During one port turnaround in New York, American Airlines invited us to a cocktail party at the Waldorf Astoria to introduce their new jet service. At the time (mid-sixties) the importance of this service did not dawn upon us. There we were, all bright-eyed and bushy-tailed, glammed-up to the eyes, drinking their champagne and eating their canapés, blissfully unaware that jet liners would soon be carrying **our** passengers through the clouds, leaving us with ghost ships.

One night ashore will never be forgotten. 11 February 1962. *Mauretania* Mediterranean Cruise and we were all on our knees. We docked at Lisbon quite late but we didn't go to bed which would have been the sensible thing to do. We got out of uniform and dollied up and off we went, clattering down the gangway just after 11p.m.

Taxis were lined up on the dock side and we piled into the first one. None of us spoke Portuguese so I used my Spanish. José was amiable and smiling and looked more like a Bank Manager than a taxi-driver. I told him we wanted to go somewhere nice, no rip-offs. He took us to one of the poshest nightclubs in Lisbon. The Manager made a big fuss of us and seated us at the best table in the restaurant. One of our Pursers, Ray Brown, looked very much like a popular film star – Ray Milland – and the Manager asked me if this was him.

'Yes,' I told him, in Spanish. 'Yes, this was him! We arrived on the *Mauretania* this morning.'

He beamed from ear to ear, clapped his hands and ordered champagne to be brought to the table. Then he signalled for the Fado singer to come and sing for us. We were launched for the night.

From there we moved on, working our way through Lisbon's sophisticated nightclubs, The Mezquita, The Machado, The Bolero to quaint old cafes and bars. Dawn was breaking when we ended up in a sleazy waterfront bar not far from the ship. We came up the gangway at 7a.m. I was clutching twelve tins of sardines and another young Purser, Ted Finch, was clutching a copper-bottomed duck! It was life-size and made of shiny metal. I don't know where he found this duck. And I don't know why I was clutching twelve tins of sardines!

It was then one mad, frantic dash to get out of glad rags into uniform and on duty. But – it can be done! The Purser's Office opened at 7.30a.m. and we were all there, gasping for coffee. The office didn't close until eight o'clock that night. I think this was one of the longest days in my sea-going career.

We had a good rapport with our shipmates. We were all in it together, just one big family, but sometimes they would play tricks. It was a quiet afternoon, mid-Atlantic, *Mauretania* and two of the three counter shutters were closed down and there were two of us on duty.

A frail, genteel lady was at the counter. She looked as if she had come straight from the hairdressing salon, not a hair out of place. She was delicately made-up and was wearing a pale blue twinset and pearls. I went to attend to her.

'What time is the Church Service on Sunday?' Her accent is cut glass from the Home Counties.

All Church notices are clearly indicated on the Purser's Notice Board outside the office but no one ever reads them.

'Which particular service did you want?' I ask.

'Anglican.'

'That's at eleven o'clock in the ...' I am being interrupted by a disgusting noise not far away. I look sideways and see my fellow Purser standing behind the closed shutter, grinning from ear to ear, with a half-inflated balloon in his hand allowing air to escape slowly!

The little lady can see only me in the office because of the closed shutters.

'Eleven o'clock in the Main Lounge. The Captain takes the Service.'

But she is no longer listening. Her eyes are riveted on me and with a curt 'Thank you,' she puts her nose in the air and walks away.

But, revenge... This handsome young Purser got his come-uppance. We knew he was entertaining an attractive young passenger so my cabin mate, I think it was Pam, and I got a length of rope from the Bo'sun – he could provide anything, that man – and made our way to the Purser's quarters late one night.

We tied the rope round the handle of his cabin door and anchored it with some authentic Girl Guide knots to the hand rail that runs the length of the corridor. He wouldn't be able to open his cabin door. No one could get out. The alternative was the porthole and the ocean outside. See if we care... But he was on duty in the office on time. Where would he (or any of us) be without friends? No one knew that we had done it.

One night Maureen and I were making our way back to the cabin. It was late. We were knackered. The world and his wife had been at the Purser's office all day. After dinner we had to go back to the office to de-code cables. As we locked up the Purser's office we had been cornered by a middle-aged, grumpy man complaining about noisy passengers next door. So we went back into the office to ring the Night Officer.

'The Night Officer and Master at Arms will investigate the disturbance, Sir.'

The bad-tempered man didn't know whether to believe us but he went on his way. Locking up once again we were surprised to see a scraggy, flimsily dressed woman fluttering along the corridor, arms waving, demanding the services of the Night Steward.

'Press the button marked 'Steward' in your cabin Madam. He will come.'

We had had enough and were longing to kick off our shoes, pour a stiff drink and collapse on to our beds. We hurried to 'A' Deck, tramped along the short corridor leading to our cabin, threw the door open and couldn't believe our eyes.

It was a shambles. The mattresses from our bunks were missing. We found them in the shower. The pillows were in the wardrobes with the sheets and blankets. We were never absolutely sure who the culprits were but on this particular evening we decided the Senior First Navigating Officer was the ringleader. We decided to wreck his bed. He was on the twelve to four watch so we timed our visit for when he would be at dinner.

The Navigators' quarters were forward, under the Bridge, and there was a walkway all around. We knew his window. It was ajar but we forced it wide open, climbed on to the handrail and got inside. The cabin was in darkness but we groped our way towards his bunk, giggling and tittering as we bumped into the coffee table and chairs on the way. Then suddenly two great brawny arms lunged at us. We screamed! Our favourite Senior First had not gone to dinner – he'd decided to have an early night!

These pranks were endemic in all Departments throughout the fleet. Safety valves? Pam and I were now back on the *Ivy* and once again we had had a hell of a day with questions. Listening is a dying art and everything has to be said twice. And sure enough the passenger would be back again the next day with the same questions. Something for them to do, perhaps.

So we were glad to get back to the cabin, put on some music. Relax with a drink. Then bed. Pam threw back the blankets and shrieked. A large, cooked lobster reposed between the sheets. The Night Steward had to be found. He could muster up anything from caviar (signature needed) to clean bed linen.

This called for serious retaliation. The Tourist Chief Steward was prime suspect. We knew he would be doing the rounds in the restaurant and bars until late – so the next evening, armed with drawing pins and a reel of black cotton we went to his cabin. Just inside the door there was a short corridor. We put two vertical lines of drawing pins, about two feet deep, waist high, on either side of this corridor. Then we wound the black cotton, criss-cross fashion, round the drawing pins so that it formed an invisible barrier. When he barged in he would bounce off this intricate gate and he wouldn't see why he couldn't get in to his cabin! And when he did he wouldn't be able to get into bed – we had fixed that too!

On the *Queen Elizabeth* it was rumoured that the Crew Purser, Des Connolly, slept on deck at night. Maureen, my cabin mate this trip, and I decided to find out if this were true. Again, we chose the right time, after dinner and before his bed time. Sure enough, there was his camp bed, on the starboard side of the forward deck, under the stars, all made up and waiting for him. So... we took one end each, marched round to the port side of the ship and left it there. We never heard a whisper about this relocation!

The ships were always at sea for Christmas and New Year. These cruises were very popular and we sailed to capacity. The *Queen Elizabeth* had an antisocial Captain on this particular voyage. He would not allow any Christmas or New Year Crew Parties. Maureen and I were rarin' to go and decided to celebrate Hogmanay. We went first-footing. We wore coats over our uniforms, threw scarves around our necks (to cover that tie). We borrowed tartan tammies from the shop and – we looked like passengers. We needed bread, a bottle of Scotch and coal. Bread was easy. Plenty of bread in the Galley. Scotch, no problem but I've no idea how we came to have a lump of coal. Perhaps a homesick Glaswegian crew member gave it to us.

We tramped all over the ship starting at the top. The Staff Captain, a very sociable animal, was ill in bed but was pleased to see us. We called on the Purser, Chief Engineer and the Doctor. We found a few Scots but not many – the majority of the crew were from Southampton or Liverpool. We made our way down and down the companionways to the bowels of the ship and arrived in forbidden territory, The Pig and Whistle, just before midnight.

The Pig and Whistle is a bare, abject space with metal pipes and shell doors. It is recreational space for the crew – their very own pub. It was heaving. Fellows singing and shouting and cheering in a thick blue haze of smoke. At the stroke of midnight we linked arms with all the Greasers, Trimmers and Deck Sailors to sing Auld Lang Syne. They were thrilled to bits that we should have found our way down there. The Master at Arms thought we were passengers and invited us to his cabin for a drink. We accepted. Our disguise must have been good or his Scotch must have been stronger than he thought!

In spite of the Captain's 'No party' Order we found quite a lot of crew parties going on around the ship and eventually got back to our cabin feeling no pain and wondering what to do next when we were invaded by the Navigators, Engineers and Electricians coming off the graveyard watch (midnight to 4a.m.) so we started all over again!

When we docked in New York at the end of one of our transatlantic voyages, the US aircraft carrier *Forrestal* was tied up at the berth opposite. Several of us were invited on board. The *Forrestal* at 75,000 tons with acres and acres of deck space, seemed like a deserted city. It carried 85 fighter planes.

We marched across the deck and were halted at a particular point. Then suddenly klaxons were blazing and there was some banging and clanging and with a jerk the grey metal deck on which we were standing was going down into the bowels of the ship. We were on a lift with no walls!

For such a big ship the alleyways and companionways were very tight and small. All grey metal. After accepting their refreshments we invited our hosts to visit *Queen Mary*. *Forrestal* was 'dry' – no alcoholic beverage – not so in our Wardroom.

We were also entertained in the most unusual place the next time we docked in New York. A British submarine had arrived. I didn't make a note of its name but it began with an 'A' and sounded like a name from Greek mythology. This long, black sinister creation was like an emaciated whale sulking in the water. We were glad to get out of uniform and into something more feminine for our visit, so we teetered across the quay in our high heels and flared skirts. We had to go through a small, and I do mean small, hatch and down sheer metal ladders. Naturally! So off came the shoes and up went our skirts!

Then we were crouching along the slender alleyways. On either side were curtained ledges. I looked behind one curtain. It was a sliver of a bunk. This is where the men slept. At the end of this alleyway was their recreation space. You could not have swung the proverbial cat around in it. So claustrophobic! So small! So stifling! And so alarming. We were shown the torpedo bays, cheek by jowl with the men's accommodation. But everything was cheek by jowl. And these submariners live down here for months and months and months without seeing daylight. I salute all submariners! It was an experience not to be missed and they were very happy to surface and visit the Wardroom of the *Queen Mary* to sample Cunard's hospitality.

My cabin mate, Julia, and I discovered that items of underwear were disappearing. We washed them and left them to dry in the bathroom opposite our cabin. Expensive French bras and lacy panties vanished. We never did find the thief.

At the same time that our underwear went missing we had another disconcerting experience. I slept in the upper berth and woke in the middle of the night to see a man standing in the cabin, a yard away from our bunks. I kept absolutely still and watched. He was slim and wearing a boiler suit. My heart was racing and yet... he just stood there staring first at the bottom bunk and then at mine then he turned and looked at clothing strewn across a chair. I don't know how long he had been there but I decided to make a move. I flung my arm outside the sheet and he was gone as swiftly and silently as he had come. The light from the corridor outside gave me a chance to see his face clearly. He was young with thick, fair, curly hair.

It happened again. Julia never heard him or saw him come or go. Always he just stood staring at our bunks and was gone like a flash the minute I moved. I reported it to the Purser who informed the Staff Captain. They wanted to identify this man, clearly a crew member, and judging by his clothes possibly from Engine or Electricians' Department. There was a crew Boxing Match on the after deck one day and I was asked to go along, mix in the crowd and keep my eyes peeled.

It was a bright, sunny day and the deck was crowded with off-duty crew but I soon recognised him. I reported to the Purser and he was identified as an Engine Rating. There were no more nocturnal visits. I pondered why on earth he would want to come into our cabin to do... nothing. Nothing but stare. But maybe he had plans? And maybe he took our underwear from the bathroom. We will never know.

Another 'weirdo' incident took place on board the *Queen Mary*. We were alongside in New York and I was in bed, off duty, and thinking about getting up. It was early – only 7 o'clock – when I heard a sort of swishing noise. It sounded like a sailor sweeping the Promenade Deck outside. Then the noise seemed to get louder. I opened my eyes and to my horror a drill was coming through the deckhead immediately above my head! I was paralysed watching this revolving, shiny metal drill above me. Then I pulled myself together, put on my housecoat and went to find the Officer of the Watch. I told him what was happening and he went off to investigate. When I got back to my cabin there was a fine pile of sawdust on my bed but the drill had gone so had the driller!

Apparently there is a huge 'loft' for want of a better word, above our Quarters known only to ship's company, of course. On closer inspection it was discovered that a hole had been drilled in our bathroom between the hot and cold water taps and then carefully plugged. So cleverly done that none of us had noticed! Next to our bathroom was a narrow alleyway for access to pipes and shafting. So... we were being watched in the bath and in bed! The holes were sealed but we never found out who had such a perverse interest in the Lady Pursers.

The *Mauretania* was away from Southampton, the base port, for six months for the winter cruising and I got caught up in the Crew Concert. Waiters, engineers, and stewards performing sketches, singing songs, dancing. Four of us, two hairdressers, a stewardess and I did the cancan. Yes, the cancan. The show was to take place on the second night in Port Said but we had to rehearse for many weeks at sea in a moving, rolling ship, cartwheels and all! One of the Pursers, Dan McWilliam, and I also sang 'Yes, we have no bananas' in Spanish! The concert was a great success.

There was always a Duty Rota on arrival in port and Southampton was no exception. Someone had to mind the ship. After we'd finished our various duties we would go 'graunching'. I don't know why this word was used. 'Graunching' means to make a crunching or grinding sound. We did no such thing. We went to let rip, eat, drink and have fun. Eight or ten of us would pile into a couple of cars (one of them was an Austin Healey Sprite) and head for the watering holes in the New Forest. We had a wild time visiting first one place then another. The Bell at Brook; the Vine at Ower; the Bugle at Hamble; the Sir Walter Tyrrell at Bursledon; the Fox and Hounds at Bursledon; the Cat and Fiddle at Walkford; the Compton Arms at Cadnam; the White Horse at Droxford... Closing time came, we were thrown out and yes, we drove back to the ship!

One night we were approaching the leafy suburbs of Southampton on a wide road with a grass verge and a broad pavement. The driver, a Navigating Officer, mounted the kerb and drove on the pavement for quite a long way until we saw traffic lights ahead. He decided to get back on to the road. This was long before Barbara Castle had thought of a breathalyser test and, of course, long before we had bumper to bumper cars on the road. At that hour roads were deserted and we never saw a soul – not even a policeman. Fortunately!

So how did we get the title of Professional Virgins? Valerie Brown and I learned of this quite by chance. We overheard a conversation between two of the Pursers.

'Thrash in my cabin tonight. But we need music.' The young, blond Purser gazed ponderously across the Square. 'We've got dollies from Tourist Class and that one, well-stacked, you know, the red-head in Cabin Class.'

'Our record player's on the blink,' the dark-haired colleague looked worried. 'We've got no music.'

'Then we'll have to borrow one,' the young blond turned away from the counter, 'We'll ask the professional virgins for theirs. But we'll have to invite them to the party as well, won't we?'

Female partygoers in uniform and collar and tie were not what they had in mind but they got the record player and the records but we cried off. Previous engagement!

So we worked hard and we played hard. Looking back through my letters and diaries I'm amazed at the hours we kept. And even

Two of the Professional Virgins (me and Valerie Brown) with passenger Pauline Koerner *Queen Mary.*

more amazed at our stamina. We were very pressured in the office, sometimes working sixteen to eighteen hours a day. We had difficult passenger problems to solve and we breathed through gills most of the time.

But sooner or later, we arrived in port, we would be off duty and we could go ashore and get away from it all. We came back like giants refreshed.

The Rich and the Famous

Before the advent of the jet plane the rich and the famous travelled by luxury liner and many chose Cunard. Management provided an Information List each voyage. It was confidential and listed regular passengers, Royalty, the aristocracy, the rich, the famous, the socially prominent. It was vitally important for expediting passengers through the formalities and for the cocktail invitations.

We also had a passenger list, a large white sheet of paper, about a yard square, prepared ashore, with the names of all passengers and cabin numbers in small print in alphabetical order. It was our working sheet and we sellotaped it flat on to the counter so that no one could take it away. We guarded this list with our lives. This was our 'Bible' for checking the passengers, ticking off each one after we had seen them and knowing who we had to chase up at the end of the muster. We had to be ever vigilant. Passengers and visitors would lean across the counter to enquire about someone's cabin number.

'Excuse me, Sir.' I edged the man's elbow clear of the list. He was already quite intoxicated, his glass of champagne tilted at an alarming angle. Any minute it would be spilt across the 'Bible.' Scotch was worse, stains more, and dark rum – watch it! Sometimes passengers just left the glass sitting on the passenger list and walked away! My list came to grief one trip when I was working in Tourist Class.

I was doing well. Lots of passengers had already been ticked off but now we were in rough weather. I had a throng of people, pushing and shoving around outside the office. Every now and again someone would dash away to be sick.

A large, lumpy lady was next. I could see she was changing colour before my eyes and yes, she vomited all over my list. That stopped the show. Seeing someone throw up usually sets others off and suddenly the Square outside the office was deserted.

The mess had to be cleared up. The bellboy got a cloth and pail of water and together we cleaned up, salvaging as best we could. Then I hung the list up to dry. I was furious. If she'd felt that ill why hadn't she moved away before? My list was ruined. Top office was waiting for numbers to send off the cable! Who had I ticked off? Who had I yet to see? I sent cards to recall many passengers whose names had been obliterated. It was a terrific work-up sorting that one out.

During embarkation reporters would be at the Purser's Office clamouring to know where so and so was berthed, who he/she was travelling with and so on. But we were ready for them. We put the letters N.P. at the side of the celebrity's name so that when we were invaded by reporters we would say that So-and-so didn't appear on the list and that he/she must have cancelled. And that got rid of the rat-pack. N.P. indicated No Publicity.

When the rich and famous travelled we didn't expect them to queue up at the Purser's Office with their completed Declaration

Form. They would be expedited using that Information List. We would make an appointment to go to their stateroom at a convenient time. This was a 'one-off' for us and I loved it.

I visited the film star Rosalind Russell, fresh from her successful film *Auntie Mame*. Her stateroom was full of gorgeous roses, she had leather luggage strewn all around but the thing I remember most was a unique toilet set on her dressing table. There was a brush, a mirror, a letter knife and a set of drinking beakers all in real tortoiseshell.

I asked for her passport and checked the details. Real name, Mrs Frederick Brisson, age, place of birth, date of birth. So we knew all the secrets. I handed the passport back to her and she smiled and asked, 'Would you like some fruit juice?'

'Yes, thank you. I would.' And I can tell you that from that day to this I have never been offered fruit juice in a real tortoiseshell beaker by anyone!

Another passenger I visited was a socially prominent Lady who moved in Royal circles. She handed me her British passport and in brackets after her name was the word 'Czarina', Russian royalty! She was Lady Zia Wernher travelling with Sir Harold Wernher, heir to the South African diamond magnate, Sir Julius Wernher, a self-made millionaire. They lived at Luton Hoo, one of the UK's most opulent stately homes now sold to become a flagship hotel. Their unique array of art treasures form The Wernher Collection at Ranger's House, Greenwich.

Vivien Leigh was unforgettable. Petite, brunette, almost ethereal as she moved around the ship. Mrs Sybil Burton, wife of Richard Burton, travelled with her children. Suzy Parker, model and film star of the Sixties, stunningly beautiful, wore not a hint of make-up.

Anthony Quinn avoided the razzmatazz in the Main Lounge each evening and liked to play chess on the deserted Promenade Deck Square.

Four of us lived in cabins on this Square tucked away beyond the shops – Garrards, Waterfords, Pringle – and there he sat, away from it all with his chosen company enjoying his game of chess with not a soul to disturb him only tired Lady Pursers trudging home to their cabins at the end of the day.

I liked to walk on deck each morning before going to the office. Once we were down there we didn't see daylight and we were breathing through gills all day. And there pounding the deck to the manner born I would see Lord Louis Mountbatten. He always nodded and smiled and said 'Good morning'.

Dame Alicia Markova, the famous ballet dancer, also enjoyed the fresh air. I would often see her on the Boat Deck, tucked up in a steamer blanket in her chair in all weathers.

Evening Safe Deposit was never a chore for me. I loved to see all those expensive baubles. A First Class passenger, Mrs Ethel Donoghue, Woolworth heiress, asked me to help fasten her necklace. She was wearing a gown of green chiffon. The necklace was emeralds and diamonds with matching earrings, brooch and ring.

Elizabeth Taylor didn't request any help. But in the Main Lounge later in the evening when I was mixing and mingling I allowed my fingers to caress her chinchilla fur stole that languished across the back of her chair. Chinchilla was said to be more expensive than mink in the Sixties. As children we, Topsy, Gordon, Monica and I, kept tame rabbits and we had a chinchilla. It had soft, dense fur, mottled grey, white underneath. Couldn't have been the same species, could it?

Viscount Montgomery had a unique experience at the Purser's Office and one that I shall never forget either! We were travelling westbound and in full cry with hordes of passengers milling around the office clutching their Declaration Forms. I spotted Lord Montgomery in the middle of this mêlée. I don't know why he was there. His name would certainly have been on the Information List. But there he was, waiting patiently with the crowd.

It so happened that we had a brand new Purser's Clerk on his first voyage and he was working at my side. I was dealing with another passenger when I heard the Purser's Clerk ask –

'And what is your occupation Sir?' (One of the questions on the form)

I looked up and met the steely blue eyes of Lord Montgomery. He nonchalantly put his left elbow on the counter, half-turned and with a wry smile said,

'Shall we say 'Soldier?'

I do want to tell you about Lillian Gish, famous film star of the silent movies. Some of you will never have heard of her, some of you will have a vague recollection of her, some of you may have seen her movies and some of you may have met her.

She was a guest at the Hostess Session, QE2, March 1977, now a small, frail woman accompanied by her Manager, Jim Fraser. She told us that she got into movies out of necessity. Her mother was widowed when Lillian and Dorothy were very small and she used to take the girls with her to the theatre simply because she couldn't leave them at home alone.

Movies needed very young faces and the lighting was terrible. Make-up non-existent. All actors and actresses played several parts in each film; for instance, she was a village belle in one scene then had to change into a cowboy's outfit in another and in yet another she was an Indian riding bareback on a horse – all distance shots.

She knew, and worked with, Mary Pickford. Her sister, Dorothy discovered Rudolph Valentino, a very reticent, handsome young man, embarrassed by the fame and notoriety which Lillian thinks had to do with his early death.

Lillian talked about her visits to England, meeting the King and Queen and Lady Diana Manners. Lillian never married and someone in the audience had the audacity to ask her why. She said that she heard so many people talking about their husbands and the disagreements between them that she realised she must not do that when she grew up.

She said that travel was the greatest education in the world and that if a gift could be bestowed upon a child she would choose curiosity – so would I.

One day I was making my way along Main Deck when marching towards me was a group of hefty men in dark suits flanking a big, sturdy man. He was a most striking figure wearing a uniform of sky-blue with gold and red chevrons, gold and red epaulettes, gold buttons. We were on collision course and there was nowhere for me to go so I flattened myself against the bulkhead.

As he marched past our eyes met and I can tell you that those eyes were the same colour as that pale blue uniform. A most impressive and unforgettable figure. It was President Tito of Yugoslavia (Josip Broz). He and his retinue had a suite of rooms on Main Deck but he wasn't seen around the ship much. He was travelling to the United Nations in New York.

Mrs Ann Ford, Marketing Director of Bear Brand stockings, was a regular traveller with her husband who was President of Bear Brand. She always brought her famous mascot with her, Chad, the teddy bear. His picture appeared on every packet of tights and stockings. He was world famous. Rather velvety, very clean and a lovely golden colour. Now this bear was absolutely priceless and was never allowed out of her sight so I was very surprised when she asked me if I would like to take Chad to my cabin overnight! It was quite a responsibility but nothing untoward happened and Chad was returned to his stateroom the next day. I believe Bear Brand was bought by Courtaulds. I wonder what happened to Chad.

The most difficult, and I do mean difficult, problem of my sea-going career presented itself on sailing day from New York. I was in the First Class Purser's Office. An attractive brunette, late twenties perhaps early thirties, came to the counter.

'I'm in Main 43. I want to change my cabin.'

A classic request. I reached for the Berthing Book, a long, thin book that registers every person and their cabin number.

'This stateroom is allocated to a couple,' I explained, 'Mr and Mrs Cameron.'

'Yes, I'm Mrs Cameron. My husband is travelling with me.' She bit her lip and glanced around the office. 'Can we talk somewhere quieter?' she whispered.

I could see that she was getting agitated so took her to the Purser's dayroom.

'You see,' she produced a handkerchief from her handbag and started to fidget with it. 'Hal and I were married in Montreal this morning. We flew to New York to embark.' She got up and paced the dayroom. 'I wanted out. I told him over and over. I didn't want to go through with it. But he wouldn't listen. I want a cabin on my own. He's paid for everything, of course but I will not share that stateroom with him.'

'Does he know?' I asked.

'Yes, but he won't agree. He doesn't listen to a word I say.'

My mind raced. Legally these passengers, presumably Mr Cameron, had contracted with Cunard to occupy that Main Deck stateroom. If we moved his wife to another cabin without his consent we would be depriving him of his conjugal rights. He could sue.

'There isn't a lot of spare accommodation.' I played for time. 'We're sailing at capacity in First Class...'

'Don't care. I'll sleep in the Lounge, if necessary.' This woman meant business. She was well-educated, lucid and sober. And I recognised a mellow Canadian accent.

'Leave it with me Mrs Cameron. I'll get back to you as soon as possible.' I needed the big guns on this. I explained the problem to the Purser. He involved the Captain and Staff Captain. The upshot was that Mrs Cameron was transferred to another cabin. Mr Cameron signed an Indemnity and confidential reports were prepared for Southampton and New York.

Believe it or not, but the next day I have a diary entry: 'And yet another inquiry and confidential reports. A man entered a female passenger's cabin in the early hours. Poor Captain Shimmin.' It concerned a Cabin Class passenger so I was not involved. Quite enough going on in top office!

Each voyage the passenger list was star-spangled and it's

impossible to tell you about them all. Here are a few – Rex Harrison and Rachel Roberts and their dog, Homer! Nancy Sinatra with her boots that were made for walking; Marjorie Proops; Michael Crawford; Richard Harris; Ludovic Kennedy; Viscount Simon; Yvonne de Carlo; Anona Winn; Count Marone Cinzano; Baroness van der Elst; Victor Mature; Charlton Heston; Paulette Goddard; Peter Sellers; Joyce Grenfell; Lawrence Harvey; Alfred Drake; Randolph Churchill; Max Bygraves; Lady Patricia Brabourn, daughter of Lord Mountbatten; Douglas Fairbanks, Helen McInnes; Leo Glenn; Lady Beamish; Muriel Spark; Pamela Frankau; Adelaide Hall; Ireneus Zuk; Groucho Marx, The Count Folke and Countess Christine Bernadotte and other members of the Swedish Royal Family; Lillian Gish, silent movie star. Mr and Mrs Bartholomew, parents of Eric Morecambe of Morecambe and Wise. Brendan Behan, Lady Guinness, David Frost, Raymond Massey; Lady Churchill; Princess Djordlaze, ex-wife of Clark Gable... I'll stop before you get bored but no one could forget the delightful, irrepressible Hermione Gingold who never, ever flew anywhere. As she constantly reminded us – flying was for the birds.

I found all these famous names were ordinary people, friendly and charming. They could relax and enjoy all the facilities in the ship away from the cameras and reporters.

And we had the 'extraordinary' passengers. An Episcopalian priest wore a T-shirt inscribed – 'And on the Eighth day God made Oklahoma.'

I was in my cabin, A.80, on the *Queen Mary* sorting paperwork during embarkation New York. It was a large cabin, en suite, with twin beds. (I had been promoted!) I slept in one and used the other to spread out my files. There was a long corridor which I used as storage space for all the prizes given away every day, reams of gift wrap paper and rolls of satin ribbon. At the end of the corridor was the porthole.

I heard a knock at the door and there stood a tall, stockily built man, with an attractive, well-dressed woman, both forty something, and two lanky young men.

'Good afternoon, ma'am.' He was American. 'Forgive me, but I wanted to see this cabin again. I didn't know it was a staff cabin.'

'Oh,' I said, 'you've obviously sailed with us before.'

'Oh yeah, ma'am!' he smiled. 'By the way, this is my wife, Julie, and my two sons, Jimmy and Joe.'

I nodded and invited them in.

'Ya see, I sailed in the *Queen Mary* when she was a troop-ship during the war and I wanted to show my family where I'd slept. And, ya see, Julie, This is it. Right here,' and he waved his arm. 'This is it,' he repeated, 'I shared this stateroom with forty men.'

After they had gone I took stock of A 80. Forty men! In here? I mentally stripped away the twin beds and furniture and all my paraphernalia in the long corridor leading to the porthole and put in rows of bunk beds. Yes, I decided, it was possible.

And a handsome African passenger at one of our cocktail parties. He had vivid blue eyes – they mesmerised me!

And there were strange goings-on. The *QE2* had just sailed from New York for the World Cruise, January 1977. A female passenger, travelling alone in an expensive stateroom was causing a stir. She was attractive, elegant, forty something. After a few drinks she was using obscene language in the public rooms. Word got around that she was paying deck sailors $1000 to go to her room. And that there was a queue! Don't believe it. Crew members are not allowed to go to passenger accommodation.

The second night after sailing, the lady in question arrived in the Restaurant for dinner, clutching a glass of champagne. She was wearing a cloudy confection of a dress, with lots of frills and flounces that could have passed as a negligée. A waiter held the chair for her.

But she stood there, smiling. Then she flicked a wispy tie belt, the clouds of chiffon fell away. She was naked.

'I can take on anyone in the whole damn ship,' she announced, waving her champagne glass. Her goggle-eyed table companions dropped spoons, knives, forks.

The Restaurant Manager reached for the telephone. Waiters scurried around with large linen tablecloths. The Master at Arms appeared like magic and escorted her away.

This was happening within hours of arriving Port Everglades and we were about to make an eighty-day voyage round the world. A big, big problem but the Captain solved it. The passenger was taken off at Port Everglades. As she was an American citizen it presented no problems from the Immigration and Customs point of view. Thank goodness her problem manifested itself before we were half way round the world!

Cases like this were not infrequent although she was the only one I saw deported. These ladies could be a problem but they usually settled to their round of parties and partners without endangering anyone but themselves with their excesses.

The Card Room next to the Library was what it said it was. A quiet room for bridge, canasta, kalooki and whist. Early in the mornings it was transformed and used for Roman Catholic Mass. One afternoon Bryan, the Social Director, burst into the office.

'Can't believe my eyes!' he grabbed the phone and punched some numbers. 'They're playing cards on the altar. Passengers are playing bridge. On the altar! Should have been stripped down after Mass at 8 o'clock this morning. What the hell's going on? Hello, is that the Second Steward's Office?'

It was great to see the names Harry and Lucy Cram on the passenger list again. They've been travelling Cunard for sixty years. This was Harry's seventy-first voyage. He doesn't remember the first. He was a baby and dines out on the story that when the ship hit bad weather in the North Atlantic he was put in a drawer of the dressing table for safety!

They lived on an island off the coast of South Carolina. When they bought the island it was infested with rats so they introduced snakes who ate the rats and then they had the snakes removed! They showed me photos of their island home, family and friends. One photo was of a portrait of his father painted by John Singer Sargent.

During one voyage Harry and Lucy were invited to the Wardroom Party and as the evening progressed someone thought it would be a good time for golf practice. I saw Harry drive a ball from the carpet of the Wardroom right through the open porthole, mid-Atlantic. Lost ball!

And I have it on good authority that Harry rode his horse into the ballroom during the South Carolina Hunt Ball!

These globetrotters had met many interesting people during their travels and it was fascinating to hear about them at first hand. Harry told me that he had met Rudyard Kipling, 'a big, energetic man', at a party in India shortly before he died in 1936.

Bill and Helen Flanagan are well-seasoned Cunard travellers. Helen was with Pan American Airlines and married Bill who had been a Navigator in B.17 bombers during the Second World War, flying out of Thurleigh, near Bedford. He has since worked on a Memorial for the 306th Bomb Group at Thurleigh.

They were placed at my table in the restaurant in the *Queen Mary*. And that friendship endures to this day. They were on board *QE2* for the Maiden Voyage when suddenly it lost its electrical power. The ship was still alongside in New York and Helen and Bill were on the open deck waving goodbye to relatives and friends who had come to their Bon Voyage party. The fact that Bill has been confined to wheels since World War II didn't matter one jot but now the elevators didn't work! How could they get down to their stateroom? Bryan, Social Director, to the rescue. He carried Bill down several flights of stairs, burst into the stateroom and they fell on to the bed laughing their heads off. Helen very relieved, walked in with the wheel chair.

I was recently invited to lunch on board *QE2* by Martha Loewenstein, another true Cunard passenger. She has been travelling Cunard since 1951 and regularly arrives in Southampton.

Margery Lee Trimble was another regular Cunard passenger placed at my table and we, too, became firm friends. She told me an interesting story over cocktails one day. She and her husband did a lot of entertaining and she told me that Joseph Conrad had been her house guest in Philadelphia in 1923. Her husband had met him during the First World War. She gave me a copy of her diary notes of his visit and I quote:

'... In spite of his sea tales he had a dread of the ocean voyage, of leaving his family and horror of publicity but his publishers, Doubledays, finally persuaded him to visit America. They were to take him on a tour of New England and end it by leaving him with us for a few days in our newly purchased home in Great Barrington... With the aid of a helpful and interested taxi driver I had scoured New York for his particular brand of French cigarettes and bought up the entire supply. He arrived on a chill rainy afternoon... when I handed him the cigarettes he sank back on to the couch and exclaimed 'My God' and actually cried with relief and pleasure. He was far from well and completely exhausted from his experiences... He had come to us on the condition that we would ask no one to meet him and we were only too happy to comply...'

Joseph Conrad died the following year on 3 August 1924 at Bishopsbourne, Kent.

Cunarder passengers were very loyal. They booked the same stateroom year after year and requested the same Steward and Stewardess. They gave parties for the ship's company which had to be sanctioned by the Captain. They kept in touch with letters, birthday cards and Christmas cards. Just one big family.

SOS ... − − − ...

Save Our Souls, a familiar and alarming call to those on the high seas. Life on board a large liner was similar to life in an elegant hotel with people wandering in and out of luxurious lounges, stepping into their equally luxurious staterooms, sitting in the splendour of the restaurant. It wasn't until you looked out of the porthole or stood on deck that you realised you were surrounded by a mighty ocean. And this defenceless liner was in the middle of it and...

There were emergencies... tense and dramatic. One Sunday night, 23 September 1962, the *Mauretania* was homeward bound from New York and to the south of Ireland when a message was received at midnight. It was from Valencia Radio Station instructing us to proceed 200 miles north to the area of a ditched Constellation plane.

Cables were coded and despatched to advise Liverpool of our diversion. Great activity went on behind the scenes as unoccupied cabins were made ready and beds in the hospital prepared. Then we received a message from the aircraft controlling rescue operations to say that our medical assistance would not be required as an aircraft carrier had arrived on the scene and we were given permission to proceed.

My diary note for Monday, 24 September reads: 'Extremely busy with SOS news of crashed Constellation in Atlantic. We got to within 15 miles and then returned to our course. Saw nothing of the rescue ships although they were on radar.'

We learned later that there were 76 American servicemen on board returning home from Germany. Meanwhile, everyday life at sea went on undisturbed for the passengers but we were late in arriving Cobh, Le Havre and Southampton with all the problems of cancelling and rearranging onward travel for the passengers.

The *Mauretania* once again came to the rescue en route New York to Naples. We stopped mid-afternoon to take an injured German seaman from a cargo ship – *Konsul Schulte* – bound for the Azores. It stood off on the starboard side and we watched as the sea boat was lowered. But there was no stretcher here. Just a group of seamen sitting in the boat. Where's the sick man? A ladder was suspended from our shell doors amidships and then one of the men in the boat promptly got to his feet and scrambled up it. His suitcase followed on the end of a rope! It was the first time I had seen the victim of a sea rescue *climb* on board. He had an eye injury and was landed at Gibraltar.

Walking on deck one evening after dinner my cabin mate, Maureen, and I stumbled across another major emergency. About a dozen deck sailors were tying thick ropes to the boat rail. 'Sea rescue, 3 a.m.,' the Bo'sun told us. They were rigging the ropes in readiness. A United States Weather Ship had a crew man with suspected appendicitis and they were going to bring him on board. We were mid-Atlantic, homeward bound.

We decided we must watch this drama so we set our alarms. Aroused from a deep sleep in a comfortable bunk in the black of night it did not seem such a good idea after all but we put on warm clothes and went to the Boat Deck. A party from the Verandah Grill was wandering about, the ladies shivering in their evening dresses and mink wraps.

Then we saw a single bright light and the weather ship crept out of the night and came in a semicircle until it was about a hundred yards away, port side. They put their deck lights on and we saw a grey ship with W.39 painted on its bows. Their lifeboat was lowered and half a dozen lights on the boat bobbed about in the choppy sea. As it got closer we realised that the lights were on the orange lifejackets of the eight men in the boat. It came slowly into our lee and we saw a man swathed in thick white blankets, roped to a stretcher.

Our deck sailors were waiting in a triangle of light in the shell doors amidships and within minutes they got a rope down to the men in the lifeboat. They tied it to the stretcher and gave the signal with a certain wave of an arm and it was hoisted slowly from the lifeboat into mid-air until it was level with the entrance to our shell doors. The stretcher swung gently, turning first one way and then the other, suspended high over the dark sea. Eager hands reached out from the yellow rectangle of light and the stretcher was pulled inside. A battered brown suitcase followed on another rope. Mission complete.

The passengers and crew gave a hearty cheer as the lifeboat sped back to the weather ship. We waited until it was back on board and then W.39 disappeared into the blackness of the night as silently as it had come. Our engines murmured and we were on our way again. It was four o'clock, we were wide awake with the adrenaline flowing so we went on the prowl to the Galley and had eggs and bacon and piping hot coffee!

And emergencies did not always happen at night. The *Mauretania* was on her way from New York to the Caribbean for a two-week cruise when one of our sailors working on deck saw a small plane crash in our wake. We circled for four hours but found nothing. Not a trace. Bermuda Triangle?

We were homeward bound on the *Queen Mary* and passengers were getting ready for the Captain's cocktail party when we altered course to assist a Greek ship – *Constantis*. It was flooded astern due to heavy seas and sinking 75 miles south with 29 men on board. We arrived at the scene early evening and the Captain decided to stand by until daylight. The cocktail party was postponed and the Bridge kept an all-night vigil.

Once again cabins were made ready. Next morning in daylight we could see this neat little cargo ship, just a spit away from us on our starboard side. It looked very small in that vast ocean. We were like a mother hen fussing over a wayward chick. During the day we received news that a tug was coming out to the ship and we sailed from the area at half past six the next morning. We heard later that she was towed into Bremen. And once again all onward travel arrangements were disrupted and had to be rearranged because of our delayed arrival. Cables to re-book flights and train tickets and hotel rooms, but it was all in a day's work for us.

We had another timely rescue shortly after the *Mauretania* had sailed from New York. During Boat Drill an elderly passenger was taken ill at his boat station. The Doctor and Nurse were summoned. The passenger had suffered a heart attack. He and his wife were transferred by our sea boat across to the *Queen Elizabeth* which was about to dock New York. He would be in a hospital within hours.

We altered course to assist a Greek ship *SS Constantis*.
Sea Rescue by *Queen Mary*
(courtesy Ocean Pictures)

All such transfers have to be documented to satisfy Customs and Immigration officials so it was all hands on deck, so to speak, to get the paper work ready in minutes to accompany these passengers and, of course, amend our own passenger manifests.

No two sea rescues are ever the same so it's always worth the effort to watch such a drama.

We had our very own emergency on board *Queen Elizabeth*. We were homeward bound – a summer sailing – and were full to capacity. I was in Tourist Travel Bureau. It was mid-afternoon with a scrum of passengers at the office when suddenly the lights went on the blink and then went out. The phone rang. I was to close the office, go to the Main Lounge and encourage as many passengers as possible to do the same.

Lights had failed in many of the public areas in Tourist Class which was now only dimly lit. The Main Lounge was swarming with passengers marching up and down, pouncing on anyone in uniform demanding to know what was going on. By now there was a strong smell of smoke, acrid and sickly. I was astonished how quickly it had permeated every room and alleyway in the ship.

But the passengers were anxious. Some were nervous. Some were aggressive. 'What the hell's going on around here?'

We told the truth. There was a small fire on A Deck near the Purser's Office. An electrical problem in a fuse box. The stewards served afternoon tea but the passengers asked again and again what was happening and we explained to them, again and again. We smiled and chatted and reassured them that everything was under control.

I stared beyond the large windows of the Main Lounge. There was nothing but endless ocean for as far as the eye could see and once again it came home to me how vulnerable we all were – in that huge liner with nothing out there but fathomless seas. The mood of the passengers became more relaxed as they responded to tea and cakes and our confident smiles and persuasion. They soon settled down and drifted away to resume their daily routine but the smell of burning was frightening and it haunted the ship for many voyages.

In bed that night I offered a prayer of thanks that the fire had broken out at three o'clock in the afternoon and not at three o'clock in the morning. Imagine that scenario! This was one of the most chastening experiences of my sea-going career.

And we had accidents on board, too. The *Mauretania* docked New York on 4 July, Independence Day. All the ships in the harbour were dressed overall so of course, we followed suit. One of the deck sailors, thirty years old and a big strong man, was fixing the flags on our main mast and fell to the deck. He was rushed to hospital in New York with multiple fracture of both legs and internal injuries.

No SOS could be ignored. Life at sea was quite unpredictable and we never knew what was beyond the horizon. Samuel Cunard's motto was – Speed, comfort and safety.

Stowaways

Stowaways were one big nuisance. They created such a lot of extra work for us and we were always stretched to the limit with our routine jobs. They came in all sorts and sizes, predominantly young and male, and were flushed out within hours of sailing, usually during Boat Drill. They come out from under wherever they have been hiding and, of course, they have no life jacket. Probably the alarm bells frighten them.

In Montreal two young men came on board as visitors and got drunk. We explained the procedure. To carry them as passengers Cunard must receive the minimum Tourist Class fare to cover the one-way passage. If this was paid they would then be accommodated in a Tourist Class cabin. A cable was sent to their next of kin and if they did not reply then the stowaways were held in the Fire Station under the beady eye of the Master at Arms.

On another occasion two nineteen-year-old male stowaways were discovered. They were Maltese and as sick as parrots before we got deep sea. They were glad to be taken off by Pilot launch.

Three female stowaways were discovered in the *Queen Mary* shortly after sailing from New York. I was summoned to the Staff Captain's dayroom to take statements from them. Two were 15 years old and one was 16. Their parents paid up and they had the time of their lives wearing only the clothes they stood up in!

Passenger ships have lots of hidey-holes but stowaways were quickly apprehended. It was a regular and irritating occurrence.

Stowaways were handed over to Immigration and Police on arrival to be deported. They were illegal immigrants, guilty of a crime and subject to the due process of law.

Canada

After a summer season on the New York run I received my first pale green envelope. Sign off on arrival and join *Ivernia*. Canada here I come!

The *Ivy* was a two-class ship carrying just over a hundred First Class and 650 Tourist passengers. A much smaller ship – 22,000 tons – and there were only two Lady Pursers – one in each Class. We sailed from Southampton and called at Le Havre, Cobh (Eire), Quebec and Montreal.

I found the Canadian Immigration documentation far more complex than that of the United States. There were so many different categories of entry documents. We had to check an A4 size card of questions for every passenger including their ethnic origin and the amount of money each was carrying. After seeing all passengers we had to compile an Alphabetical Book – our precious 'A' Book. It was a similar exercise to the large manifests we prepared for the Americans except that this was required in book form.

There were enormous numbers of immigrants from Europe and I remember in one particular muster of six hundred passengers less than half a dozen spoke English!

On one such trip I was confronted by a large family ranging from a tiny baby in arms to Grandma, all staring at me with doleful brown eyes, bewildered by the ritual of question and answer. All went well until I got to the address whence they had come. They had given one word only and I knew this would not satisfy the Canadian Immigration Officers on arrival. All attempts to find out where this place was 'near' failed so I called in Terps. Our Interpreter, Frank Necas. A distinguished, portly diplomat who was in the wrong place at the wrong time when the tanks rolled into Prague. Exiled from his wife and family he made his home on the Cunarders along with the rest of us.

Frank discovered that this family lived on a tiny island off the coast of Greece and they had been the only inhabitants until their decision to start a new life in Canada!

It was an exciting time in the *Ivy*, through the ice-fields. Additional watches were kept on the Bridge and we often saw US Coastguard planes on ice patrol, bombing the icebergs and growlers. These icebergs were indescribably beautiful in the early morning sun, like a pink wedding cake on an ice-blue tablecloth.

We often got into foul weather as we followed a more northerly route than that of the *Queens*. The Captain stayed on the Bridge and slept in a small cabin aft of the wheelhouse.

There were many seasick passengers. Lots of sawdust needed. This was provided by Stairhead men – stewards with buckets of sawdust. It was sprinkled wherever necessary but the top and bottom of a flight of stairs seemed to be the most popular place for a mishap.

I was sorry for these passengers who couldn't understand how we stayed mobile during the storms. They really felt so wretched they wanted to die. The only advice I could give them was to wrap up warmly, go topsides and watch the horizon – yes – there it is going, going, gone and here it comes back up, up, up again. And eat apples!

We were all good sailors and I can remember only one girl who resigned because of her seasickness. There may have been others but we really couldn't afford to go sick. There were hundreds of passengers to interview, passports and visas to check then a ton of typing to be done.

One afternoon we were in the thick of a Force 10 about two hundred miles from Father Point Light vessel. I have the Log Card – they were printed as souvenirs for passengers every trip – and it reads: 'SW storm (force 10) very rough seas, very h'y SW swell, overcast. Reduced speed 25 hours.'

Light vessels are stationed at the entrance to harbours. For the St Lawrence it is Father Point; for New York it is Ambrose. Bishop Rock off the Scilly Isles means that we have found England and for Southampton it is Calshot Spit. They were a welcome beacon for us after thousands of miles of ocean.

I was typing manifests when the ship rolled (later confirmed as 21 degrees). I gripped the edge of the desk but the typewriter and I crashed to the deck in a deluge of heavy metal, papers, pens and rubber stamps. I was lucky to get away with a whopping blue-black bruise the length of my right thigh. The gales persisted and we closed the office. The Captain changed course to get out of the storm and the next morning we learned that we had been without radio and radar during the night!

In the smaller ships, such as the *Ivy*, we had an additional duty. Tape Duty. The aim was to have mood music playing softly throughout the ship before dinner. The Assistant Purser was responsible for putting on the correct tape – the one advertised in the Daily Programme. OK. But the equipment was such that it only played for forty minutes and the tape had to be turned to play the second half of the concert. I was never convinced that passengers were listening or even noticed the music but we got bawled out again and again because we forgot to 'Turn the Tape' and hundreds of unfinished classical concerts were left in limbo on the North Atlantic.

The trip along the St Lawrence River was unforgettable, especially during the Fall. Hundreds of miles of waterway flanked by a tapestry of gold, bronze and sepia. Quite beautiful.

During one trip, shortly before arrival Quebec, a Greek passenger became ill. Suspected smallpox! We anchored in the river and hoisted the yellow quarantine flag. The Port Health Doctors sought another opinion. Two Professors from McGill University came on board but were unable to agree on the diagnosis so the Medical Chief from Ottawa was flown to Quebec.

Passengers gave us hell at the Purser's Office. Others tramped the deck getting more and more angry with the delay. They wanted to be ashore. Chickenpox was diagnosed and a big cheer went up as clearance for the ship to dock was granted.

Later that day the Captain asked me to go ashore with letters to post. He told me not to change out of uniform but to wear my hat. At the bottom of the gangway two handsome, smart, crisp men of

The Royal Canadian Mounted Police were on duty. To my amazement they stood to attention and saluted as I stepped ashore! Now I have never been saluted at before. I have never been in the Forces. I didn't know *how* to salute. What to do? So I just looked first at one, then the other, smiled and went on my way feeling rather important. It's not likely to happen again but you never know your luck in a big city!

From Quebec we sailed on to Montreal, our final port. End of westbound voyage. We docked on a Friday and sailed on the Monday or Tuesday – a long weekend. Such luxury after the rat-race of one night in New York! Of course, there was the port duty rota but we all got some time off and passengers would invite us to dinner or to their log cabin on the shores of a lake in the Laurentian Mountains. We would arrive in the moonlight. And what bliss to wake up to the smell of pine forests and look across the placid lake and listen to the silence.

During the winter months when the St Lawrence was frozen and closed to passenger shipping, our port of call was Halifax, Nova Scotia. The coldest place I've visited. Dairen in The People's Republic of China is a close second. The wind was razor sharp, the snow was deep and solid but the Nova Scotians offered very warm hospitality.

I have a recollection of a group of us marching back to the ship late one night after a party. We were crunching through thick snow along railway lines. It was dark and we were feeling no pain, singing at the tops of our voices. It was the unauthorised version of 'Colonel Bogey' – led by one of our Pursers, Alex Hunter-Robertson, a former Royal Marine.

'Hitler, he only had one ball;
Goering's were only very small;
Himmler's were very similar;
But poor old Goebbels had no balls at all,

da..did...da...da...da.' and so it went on.

We didn't feel the jagged edges of that wind cutting our cheeks as we reeled and stumbled and tripped along the railway lines, quite oblivious to the danger of a train hurtling towards us. But we didn't get mowed down and we didn't get locked up for trespassing! I have no idea how or why we came to be marching along those railway lines to get back to the ship.

Each Class had its own shop and shop assistants – Renee, Fay, Ruth – the Candy Kids – and they organised a party. A Burial Service for my old uniform hat. This was the night before arrival Le Havre, homeward bound. We congregated in the 'R' Deck cabin and a very noisy funeral party made its way to the after end led by one of the stewards dressed as a preacher. I was swathed in a blanket like a mummy, arms and legs completely immobilised, with my hat firmly on my head.

About six men carried me and then held me out horizontally over the stern. Sure enough the wind snatched off my hat and it was never seen again. I can see to this day the frothy, white churning waters from the propellers a short distance below my head! I was 'unwrapped' and we all did the Conga round the ropes and bollards back to the 'R' Deck cabin – the party continued...

Looking back this was highly irresponsible and dangerous but we were nearly home after a tough voyage – one false move and I would not have been writing this.

Cobh – Cobb H as we called it, was a unique port to visit tucked under green hills with its white-washed cottages. Winds and currents were tricky at the entrance to the harbour. On Saturday, 29 September 1962 my diary says 'We ran into heavy weather this afternoon. Hove to off entrance to Cobh harbour. A few cross-channels (passengers) to worry about.' The next day 'the Pilot boarded but we were hove to all day. Church Service as usual. Eventually entered harbour 5.30p.m. Sailed 8.30p.m.'

The local women came on board with their hand-knitted woollens and shillelaghs to sell, not forgetting the bottles of Irish whiskey. It was great fun dealing with the Irish who seemed not to have a care in the world whatever hour of the day or night we docked. After sailing I would go on deck to smell the peat from the mainland. It gave such a good, earthy sense of natural wellbeing.

The pressure really piled up cross-channel after sailing from Le Havre. Homeward bound... The Channels... Obligato Night... and so much work! One trip I was asked to go down to the Crew Purser's Office to help with the telex about crew wages. Southampton was waiting for the details for pay-off. 'Down' really did mean down steep metal companionways, along bleak alleyways to an office that looked like an old metal filing cabinet.

I was engrossed in the lists of figures when I heard a commotion in the alleyway. I looked up and saw a bride in a long white dress, with a bouquet, on the arm of a handsome groom, followed by a retinue of noisy shipmates. They disappeared in the direction of the Pig and Whistle.

'Are the crew having a Fancy Dress Party for Obligato Night?' I asked.

'No,' the Crew Purser said, 'it's a Queer's Wedding.'

I enjoyed my posting to the *Ivy*. Those Canadian Immigration cards and that 'A' Book were a real slog and the weather was often tumultuous but it was a dramatic route to sail with the storms, the icebergs, the Coast Guard planes overhead, the navigation of the St Lawrence and all those wonderful shipmates and passengers to share it with.

This posting clinched my future with Cunard. About a year after joining I met a man, James Fraser Brooks, and I knew that this was the one. He proposed and we decided to marry which meant that I would have to tender my resignation from Cunard once plans were finalised. I sailed again in the *Ivy* but received a telephone call when we arrived at Le Havre to say that he was dangerously ill and I should return to UK immediately. It so happened that the *Maurie* was due in Le Havre homeward bound for Southampton that evening and I was transferred and returned to England as a DBS, Distressed British Seaman on board the *Maurie*.

On docking I travelled to Grantham Hospital immediately and got there in time but this fine young man, with such a promising career ahead of him, died at the age of 24. Cunard gave me generous compassionate leave and I eventually returned to sea, scarred and flawed, but surrounded by shipmates who got me back on track and functioning again by their friendliness and silence. They never referred to my loss but they must have known – the *Ivy* sailed one short on that fateful voyage to Canada. And so I dedicated myself to this work and all the things I am telling you now.

Naples

In the mid-Sixties the Company decided to base the *Mauretania* in the Mediterranean. Naples would be our home port instead of Southampton. This was a confident yet daring decision intended to attract passengers from the heart of Europe for New York. I was posted there – and to my astonishment I was promoted to Senior Assistant Purser.

As all Cunard officers know the promotion ladder is long and steep with very few drop-outs on that clearly-defined ascent. The Navigating Officers spend years and years waiting for a step up – and every one of them held a Master's ticket on the day they joined the Company.

For Lady Pursers the promotion ladder was almost non-existent. I was told to wear another half inch of gold braid on my sleeves. My salary was increased and so were my responsibilities. Training and control of Lady Pursers. And I had a spacious stateroom with twin beds, bathroom and shower en suite. A far cry from the 'B' Deck aft, with upper and lower bunks on my first trip!

I had a table of eight passengers in the First Class Restaurant and learnt the art of steering conversation away from discussions on Jews, Gentiles and politics.

The administration had quite a different flavour. I spent much more time with the passengers, mixing and mingling, listening for any hint of complaint or unhappiness. And I worked longer hours. The Daily Programme was chock full of events and competitions ranging from Bridge Tournaments to Children's Gymkhanas which meant that the right entry forms and paper work had to be in the right place at the right time with the right prizes. All winners' names are published at the end of the voyage and it was important to record these accurately for the Printer.

I was responsible for getting all prizes from the shop. These are ordered by a signed chit, no money is handled. Then all prizes have to be gift-wrapped and bowed. Many a midnight have I got back to my cabin to wrap and bow prizes for the next day's events before crashing into bed. But after the razzmatazz of the crowded, smoky Lounges and music it was quite therapeutic to sit fiddling about with satin bows in the middle of the night! Sometimes I could inveigle a willing shipmate to have a session of bow-making on a quiet afternoon and that helped enormously.

We gave lots of prizes away, every day, every evening. There were dance prizes in the Main Lounge. The couple under the centre light when the music stopped each received a beautifully wrapped and bowed prize.

'Congratulations,' I beamed and went to dig out the next set of prizes from my deep carrier bag behind the stage.

'Say, ma'am.' The prize-winner had followed me. He was clutching the wrapping and a quality hair brush. 'What the hell am I supposed to do with this?'

The man didn't have a hair on his head!

I devised a colour code of wrapping paper so that this didn't happen again. We chose 'sexless' gifts from the shop. Travel clocks, small Royal Crown Derby china dishes, cake knives, model ships and sailor dolls in a dark-blue velvet uniform with the name of the ship on the white cap.

I needed the Purser's signature on the certificates given with the prizes for the various events – at least 20 winners and 6 runners-up each crossing.

Of particular importance was the large number of passengers travelling alone. We organised cocktail parties for them to meet and I visited every one of them in their stateroom. If they were out I would leave a card saying that I had called and that they could contact me via the telephone exchange should they wish to discuss anything. This meant that I had to be ready with a listening ear any time of the day or night. I would check with the Sister for anyone in hospital so that I could send a Get-well card – and visit.

Another important task after sailing was to comb through the manifest for birthdays. Every passenger with a birthday during the voyage received a birthday card signed by the Captain and a birthday cake made by the Chef. We also needed to know the number of children travelling so that we could get sufficient prizes for their events, not forgetting sweets for their Tea Party. In addition prizes for the Fancy Head Dress Parade had to be gift-wrapped and bowed!

Before arrival in each port, the prize account had to be balanced and all unused prizes returned to the shop to be bonded for Customs inspection. They stayed in that sealed locker until we were clear of territorial waters after sailing when we would indent for supplies again.

Staff Table seating lists were important. The Senior Officers wanted to know the names of passengers at their tables and I needed them for the cocktail invitations. On one voyage New York to Naples we had a most unusual group of passengers. One hundred nuns and forty priests. And thereby hangs a conquest...

As you will realise with so many attractive passengers on board and so many parties our officers were in great demand. They had a secret type of Karate Club. Belts were awarded for various conquests. The highest award went to the officer who bedded a woman travelling with her husband. But here was a new challenge. The highest award this trip would go to the officer to bed a nun. Proof was needed by

We gave lots of prizes away – *Mauretania*
(courtesy Ocean Pictures)

producing a pair of panties or bra. One of our Pursers claimed the top award and produced a pair of panties to prove it!

For my part I found the nuns gentle and charming. They were teachers or nurses and drank ginger ale at the cocktail parties. The priests had stronger stomachs.

Before arrival Gibraltar I would give a Shopping Talk. The Liquor Store was on the top of everyone's list but there were many other interesting things to buy – perfumes, leather goods, silk scarves.

The Naples run was a hell of a slog. We had four ports in the Mediterranean. Naples, Genoa, Cannes and Gibraltar. Two ports on the same day – Genoa 8a.m. and Cannes at 7p.m! All passengers to muster, manifest, process for immigration, and balance. We were whacked before we set off deep sea for New York. The Italian documents were complex and difficult because they were in Italian – naturally! And the Immigration and Customs Officers were quite demanding. It was well known that the ship's Ways and Means Committee often had to cough up for a speedy clearance. With my own eyes I saw just how we got those pieces of paper rubber-stamped.

I remember this big, perspiring Customs Officer (I've never seen a small Customs Officer). The Purser was there to deal with him and lo and behold this big hulk of a man rolled up his left trouser leg. He was wearing thick, black woollen knee socks – in that heat – Naples, mid-summer! He slipped a carton of 200 cigarettes down the inside of one black sock and then rolled up the other trouser leg and stuffed another carton down that one. He stood up, shook one leg then the other and the ship was cleared and everyone was happy. I had to suppress giggles. I could imagine him clumping down the gangway with those cartons knocking against his knees!

And if you didn't play? Well, a ship could be hanging about for hours, with coaches on the quayside waiting to take passengers on their excursions, stores to be loaded, everything went awry. I know from my recent experience on cargo ships in far-flung ports that Masters have a tough time assuaging appetites of port officials.

One morning in Naples I went ashore to do some shopping and walked into a tremendous commotion on the quay-side. Police cars, ambulances, cranes, hordes of workmen. Apparently a car with several people in it had driven into the dock. All drowned. I did not get involved. I didn't see a thing. In the midst of life...

During one of our port turn-arounds in Naples the ship was repainted overall. She looked terrific. Everybody admired our fresh, clean look. We sailed up the coast to Genoa, our next port. Captain Treasure Jones went off in the Agent's car to do some business and on his return he, too, stood to admire the new look of the *Maurie*. His eyes travelled down to the waterline. He did a double take. The Italians had painted over the Plimsoll line! He pounded up the gangway to find the Chief Officer who went berserk. Maritime Law requires every ship to sail with the Plimsoll Line clearly marked. The Landing Agent had to find a team of painters before we could sail!

But Italy was wonderful and there were rewards for all the slog and the long hours and frustrating delays and all the multi-buffone. A word invented in the Purser's Office. It is used to this day by Patrick Fison, one of our Pursers!

On arrival Naples replacement crew would arrive by chartered plane and crew members due for leave would fly home later that day. These hand-over days were riotous. Two Pursers accompanied the crew to the airport to streamline their departure through Italian immigration. The crew going on leave couldn't be contained and sometimes we had to pour them on to the plane.

There were organised tours to Rome but one of our jaunts came to an abrupt end for one passenger. She was an elegant, mature American lady travelling with her husband. We were in the foyer of the opulent Hotel Quirinale with its high-domed ceilings. This lady fell to the marble floor and remained there clearly in great pain. A doctor was summoned and arrangements were made to get her to a hospital immediately. Passport and proof of identity needed. American Consul notified. She had to stay overnight but fortunately the ship's doctor was able to convince the hospital authorities that she was fit enough to return to the ship by car the next afternoon in time for sailing.

I couldn't believe my eyes when I saw her on board. Her right arm was clamped cross her chest with just her finger tips visible under her left arm pit. She was covered in plaster from neck to waist. I don't know how she could breathe! Back on board our hospital soon winkled her out of the casing and made her comfortable. What was I saying about never being off duty?

Two Senior Pursers, Bryan Vickers, Peter Irvine and I were off duty and decided to go by local transport to Pompeii, just a stone's throw from Naples. It rained all day but I wouldn't have missed seeing this ruined city. It nestles at the foot of Mount Vesuvius and was buried by an eruption on 24 August AD79. Excavations began in the first half of the eighteenth century and have revealed streets and houses and its citizens fossilised in volcanic ash. The awful suddenness of the tragedy is obvious all around with rows of ruined houses like decaying teeth with men and women and children sitting in doorways, lying on the ground, clutching bowls covered in molten ash. They look like unfinished sculptures. And the work goes on exposing a network of straight streets paved with large cobble stones. Grooves in these stones were said to have been made by the chariot wheels. Squares, temples and theatres, workshops and stores all found a new life, resurrecting the scene on that August day long ago.

Pompeii was the residential suburb of Naples where the rich merchants had their villas. There are no windows to the houses but the roofs are open to let in the light. In some houses the opening in the roof is adorned by gargoyles which act as fountains when it is raining. The rain water is caught in a spout and comes through the mouth of the gargoyle to a square pool in the main hall below. The houses have lofty halls with marble pillars. Outside are gardens and courtyards with Ionic pillars, statuettes and flowers. Certainly a rich man's playground.

The walls of the houses, in particular that of the bachelor Vetti

Brothers, are painted throughout depicting various scenes. One room was locked but the guide sidled up to my two shipmates and there was a whispered conversation. The guide nodded and grinned, reaching for the bunch of keys dangling from a chain on his trouser belt. He opened the door and we were ushered inside.

It is a large oblong room with a vivid mosaic floor. The walls are covered with well-preserved painted friezes depicting naked men and women scrambling all over each other. Orming! It's a Lincolnshire dialect word meaning climbing about. Clumsily. Clearly a good party was in full swing and had been captured for posterity. I saw various jars and vases and artefacts on small tables and ledges around the room. They were all phallic in design.

When we got outside I asked, 'What did that guide say to you before he opened up for us?'

Bryan and Peter looked at each other, eyebrows raised.

'Clearly he doesn't show it to everyone.' I said. 'That was a highly-privileged locked room, not for general consumption and you can see why it's kept locked.'

'He wanted to know if you were Peter's wife,' Bryan confessed. 'And we said 'yes'. Otherwise you would not have been allowed in!" And they both exploded in laughter.

'Well my education has been advanced somewhat thanks to the Vetti Brothers. I've never seen anything like it. Need a cup of coffee after that, let's go.'

Once again the Agent had put a car at the Captain's disposal but he didn't want to go ashore so he offered it to those of us who did. We headed for the famous Amalfi Drive. It climbed up and round and round mountainous hairpin bends past olive groves, vineyards, lemon groves and it was here on the Amalfi Drive that I picked my first orange from a tree. The road was a ledge hewn into the rock with a sheer drop to the rocks and blue-green sea below.

Sorrento stands sheer out of the sea with great cliffs rising from the narrow beach. White houses set amongst flowering shrubs and gardens.

Positano is quaint. It only has one street and the houses are in tiers. Steep stairways lead down to the beaches. From Positano the road follows the coast closely to Amalfi where fisherman mend their nets, paint their boats and mind their own business.

Salerno brought back wartime memories for one of our shipmates. Harold Grimes was in the Royal Navy during the war and his ship was anchored in the bay of Salerno for three weeks at the height of the fighting. He told us that a fellow officer, standing at his side just disappeared. He was blown to smithereens. It's difficult to believe that this beautiful coast with its sheer rocks and cliffs and blue-green sea witnessed such ravages of war.

The islands of Capri and Ischia were wonderful retreats, away from it all for the day. And then there was the San Carlos Theatre. We got tickets for 'Rigoletto' and piled into a box next to the Royal Box. We were a bit crowded – there were ten of us. The box was for five! Odd numbers breathe in, even numbers breathe out but it was too special to miss.

I loved the spaghetti run, and we sailed with good numbers but along came the ultra-modern Italian liner *Michelangelo* to woo the passengers with its distinctive lattice-work funnel. The *Maurie* seemed very stuffy in comparison and we were soon back in Southampton. We couldn't compete.

It goes without saying that we enjoyed a high degree of job satisfaction. We were all part of a well-organised team, all working together and all with the knowledge that the work just had to be done, come what may, as 'we dock in the morning.' Anything could and did happen.

Cruising

There were two cruise liners in the Cunard fleet when I joined the company. *Caronia* and *Mauretania*. The *Caronia* – the Green Goddess – was built as a dual-purpose liner for luxury cruising and Atlantic crossings but she spent most of her time cruising the world from New York.

Both ships carried two Lady Pursers and we longed to be sent to one of them but we had to puke our way across the North Atlantic for about two years before our turn came. One day I arrived Southampton to find that familiar pale green envelope waiting for me. Sign off and join *Mauretania* for winter cruise season in the Caribbean. Yes, Sir. We sailed from Southampton mid-December. During the westbound Atlantic crossing the Purser said the Captain wanted to see me and together we went to his dayroom. Captain Jones told me that he had received information that the Venezuelan pilot at La Guaira did not speak English and that I would be required on the Bridge to interpret the orders from the Pilot when we docked there in March. I was surprised that so much advance notice was needed for pilots and docking in ports around the world.

I had never had to translate or interpret any nautical language and what is more, I only had a hazy idea of what was said on the Bridge, so this was another awesome challenge. Get it wrong and we could be parked in Plaza Mayor, La Guaira.

I was released from afternoon duty in the Purser's Office to spend time with one of the Navigating Officers, Glynn Parry. He explained to me exactly what happens when a ship is brought alongside.

'The Pilot boards the ship approximately one mile north of the breakwater. Usually three tugs are available. It is important to establish which rope is to be used – ship's or tug's.'

He went on to tell me about the engine commands – stop, slow, half or full speed, ahead, astern. Leeward. Windward. Then there are the orders for – send rope ashore – don't send rope ashore – position of ship on pier – the gangways – make fast – and thank goodness... finish with engines.

As my good shipmate took me through all this I realised that most of the commands were in the imperative. Not my favourite verb conjugation. Suddenly I wanted to go home! But with his invaluable help I made notes of all the technical terms and phrases and studied them in my cabin, in the library, on deck. I had to get it right.

Fortunately time was on my side. It was about eight weeks before we were due to dock La Guaira.

New York was the base port for the cruises to the Caribbean islands during the winter months. Every two weeks we sailed, full to capacity, carrying passengers to the magical islands. It was hectic. If we thought mustering two thousand passengers in five days on the North Atlantic was tough going we quickly learnt that we had to prepare manifests for about eight hundred passengers in less than forty-eight hours. We had a six o'clock call to be on duty every morning for six months. We survived, of course, and there were compensations. We often left New York in a snow storm and within hours we would be in tropical sunshine.

We arrived at a different island every day, each with its own particular requirements – number of forms, number of copies, Customs control – all to be complied with before the ship was cleared and passengers were allowed ashore. Some Immigration Officers wanted six copies of the manifest, others eight, others ten. These documents were prepared by what was affectionately known as the Chain Gang and we took over the Cabin Class Nursery. A group of Pursers were ensconced here compiling the manifests and all paper work needed at each port of call. On the Atlantic this work was done in the Purser's Office but the pressure and urgency was such that we needed a quiet office with no interruptions from passengers or telephones.

So the Chain Gang worked like stinkum, shut away in this large converted office but it was a good and happy team. Checking, sorting, writing and typing, day after day. And it was possible to loosen up a bit – we had no passengers to deal with, no one could hear what we were talking about. We could work without jackets and no one could see that we had kicked off our shoes. Away from the strict protocol of the Purser's Office we could eat and drink tea or coffee.

There was a Port Duty Rota and we would dash ashore, usually a group of Pursers, Navigators, Engineers – in fact, whoever was lucky enough to be off duty – and head for a beach. It didn't matter which one. They were all beautiful and deserted. Bone white sand with water of peacock blue. Now there are high-rise luxury hotels where there used only to be a thatched cabana or two dotted about for shade.

The Straw Market at Kingston, Jamaica, near the waterfront was a splendid babble of noise and colour with smiling, lumpy women selling their showy creations. We quickly soaked up the atmosphere and sunshine and people and happiness of it all.

We left Kingston and drove on a good tarmac road flanked by sugar plantations and soon arrived at Montego Bay on the north coast. It was fabulous and made even more fabulous for us because a socially-prominent, rich and famous, regular passenger, Harvey Firestone, had put his villa at our disposal for the day. Cool rooms, shaded verandah and a few steps to the beach. That was living, that was...

Haiti had its own particular magic for me – it must be that voodoo. A gang of us went to a nightclub and saw weird figures yelling and leaping with wild abandon. They carried flaming torches and flashing knives and the ritual ended with the sacrifice of a live cockerel.

The entrance to the Iron Market is a remarkable construction. It looks like a grand Victorian railway station. An arch supporting four turrets with balconies capped by domes and a clock in the centre. All around this grand entrance it is a stinking shambles. Stalls selling everything from beads to bananas next to heaps of foul-smelling rubbish. Crowds of people and dogs everywhere. And the most abject poverty. Haiti is often in the news today and still I see those foul-smelling heaps of rubbish on the television.

According to a recent issue of *Newsweek* two-thirds of the labour force is unemployed and six out of every ten people are malnourished. Nothing has changed. But they have big smiles and welcome visitors.

I hurried on my way to rendezvous with my shipmates at Bar Carlos, al fresco, where we sat in the shade drinking the most wicked Planter's Punches imaginable. Most bartenders in the Caribbean have their own recipe for a Planter's Punch. I don't know what Carlos put in his but I refuse to be held responsible for the effects! It is said that I was in the rear seat of the taxi on the way back to the ship with my right toe in the taxi-driver's right ear – but you know what shipmates are!

Martinique – jasmine, orchids, frangipani and scarlet bougainvillea. The humming bird doesn't know where to start. This is the home of the *merengue*, that rhythmic dance inspired by the slaves who, heavily chained and shackled, developed a side shuffle, dipping the knee and dragging the foot as they sang to that rhythm. Trinidad in carnival time. Curacao, clean and neat and Dutch. We went to the Piscadera Bay Club and it was here that I learned to snorkel and saw the wonderful underwater world of fish of the most exquisite colours and shapes.

Barbados – producing sugar cane for commerce and paradise for the holidaymakers. Paradise Beach was deserted with not a hotel in sight! On to Grenada – a lush island with misty woods and fertile plantations. A community of thrifty farmers cultivating cinnamon, nutmeg, cloves, ginger, mace, tonka beans.

We bought rum in St Thomas, Virgin Islands. It was cheaper than the Coca-Cola we bought in New York! We weren't allowed to bring booze on board but we got around that by taking a plastic bottle of fruit juice ashore then we would buy white rum (3s 6d = 17.5p a bottle) and decant it. Sometimes there were spot checks by the Officer of the Watch at the gangway but I didn't get caught.

We had big plans for our visit to Mexico. Two days in port and overland tours to supervise. We anchored off Vera Cruz and passengers were taken ashore by launch. Vera Cruz is the oldest of Mexico's colonial settlements and its buildings exude a mellow confidence. This is where Hernan Cortes came ashore and launched his campaign in 1519.

And this was one of the most exhilarating and exhausting tours we made. A group of fifty-two passengers went by chartered plane for a two-day visit to Mexico City, returning overland.

I am up at five o'clock, mustering the group in the Main Lounge at seven o'clock for Mexican Immigration and then ashore by launch.

A coach is waiting to take us to the airport. The plane squatting on the tarmac is so *small* but, of course, exactly right for our numbers. I counted heads again and follow the last passenger on to the plane. The cockpit is 'open' and the pilot is visible to us all. After a little more delay – remember we are in *mañana* country – the engines rev and just as the door is being closed a youth in shorts and a flapping white shirt hurls himself into the plane and lands in a heap on the floor near the pilot. I have no idea who he is but he gave me a broad smile and got a free ride to Mexico City on Cunard's charter plane.

On arrival at the Del Prado Hotel rooms were allocated and we were all glad to unwind and relax after such an early start. I had not been in my room ten minutes when the phone rang. The receptionist tells me that one of our passengers demands to see me. I go down to the foyer. It's Mrs Unwin, a forty something American. She is angry and agitated.

'My room is a disgrace. I don't like it. In fact, I don't like Mexico City (we arrived less than half an hour ago).' She lit a cigarette and puffed smoke into the air. 'Please arrange for me to fly back to the ship. At once!'

I took a deep breath.

'Certainly, ma'am. I'll make some enquiries. Please take a seat.' She sinks into a deep leather settee in the corner of the foyer and I go over to the desk.

The attractive young receptionist must have heard the out-pouring. She's already thumbing through a brochure. Then she picks up a phone and there is a rapid machine-gun firing of Spanish.

'*Gracias*,' she put the phone down. 'The evening flight to Vera Cruz is fully booked. I'm sorry.'

'Thank you,' I return to Mrs Unwin. She's lighting her second cigarette. I explain the position to her.

'I'm afraid there's nothing more we can do at the moment. I'll check the flight situation again before dinner. So why don't you go to your room and order some coffee. Rest awhile.'

'OK.' She scoops up her handbag and moves to the lift.

I never heard another word from her.

I find this a good cure-all for hysterical and not so hysterical complaints and wobblers that passengers throw at me at all hours. They are hot, tired, hungry and thirsty – and may have had a quarrel with their husband before seeking me out. A little period of rest and quiet works wonders.

Mexico City is 7,450 feet above sea level and was built on an island in a great lake. It is said that the city is sinking and the Latin American Tower is built to float on the underground mud! It was crowded and noisy and the traffic was a nightmare.

The next morning we piled into a touring coach and the first stop was at the Shrine of Guadalupe. Women of all age groups were on their knees making slow and painful progress across the wide paved Plaza. Some of them had children with them. They were walking just a step in front of their mothers. What devotion! What penance!

Soon we were passing slum-ridden suburbs, speeding along a highway and then we were gazing in awe at the ancient pyramids of Teotihuacan built around AD300 by an unknown race. The pyramids have a pleasing symmetry and much carved stonework depicting serpents and fierce gargoyles. I was amazed that the colours had retained their vividness. The decoration on the lower walls is now pink. In AD300 it would have been red, a natural dye from the dried body of the female cochineal insect *coccus cacti*. The cochineal is also prevalent in Peru and was used widely by the pre-Columbian civilisations for dyeing textiles and decorating ceramics.

The return by coach was an interesting but tiring ride along dusty roads, passing through untidy, scruffy little villages where the only traffic was mules and chickens and dogs. The barefoot children stared back with their huge dark eyes as our coach left them nothing but clouds of swirling dust.

At times the countryside was like a desert, at others there were small farm settlements surrounded by pastures, trees and scrub with lazy men astride lazy donkeys. Thick pine forests stretched away to mountains and snow-capped volcanoes in the distance. Everywhere I saw the maguey (agave) cactus. Tequila is made from the distilled juice of this plant.

At a comfort stop I went over to a clump to get a closer look. It is about three feet tall with large, fluted green spikes reaching in all directions. I was amazed how hard and vicious the spikes were. Later in the day I was introduced to the ritual drinking of tequila – I have a vague recollection of salt and limes and crystal clear liquid that nearly blew my head off.

We had lunch at the town of Puebla sprawling across a broad valley with Popocatépetl rising to the west. Here the speciality was tiles and pottery and ceramics and the locals were not disappointed. The passengers were good customers. Then we hurried down to Vera Cruz arriving at 8p.m. to find that the launch service had been temporarily suspended because of the high winds.

That evening a group of us went ashore to relax and unwind visiting bars and a nightclub. We wended our way back to the dock to get the launch to the ship. It was a balmy evening and no one was in a hurry. We passed many street vendors, old men, youths, old women, young women, children – selling their wares, everything from serapes, silver, onyx to plastic toys and celluloid windmills.

Sitting on the side of the road was this young and beautiful woman, a faded shawl draped around her shoulders. Thick jet black hair was swept back in braids. Several children scrambled around her. Anxious dark eyes beseeched us to stop and buy. She held up carved onyx bookends. Beautifully crafted work. I bargained with her, beating her down relentlessly. I could afford to pay the price she asked but it was like a battle of wits and I eventually bought the bookends. Then she stood up to wrap them in old newspaper and I could see that she was heavily pregnant.

Here we were, a gang of pixillated shipmates in the early hours of the morning, in a street in Vera Cruz arguing with this woman about a dollar or two when she and those children should have been at home and in bed. In that moment I hated myself. And I was ashamed. But I learnt an important lesson after my visit to Vera Cruz.

More recently, ashore in South America, I see heavily pregnant women, surrounded by children, still trying to sell things by the roadside to get money for food for their families. Nothing has changed. But I have never bargained with any street vendor since that experience in Vera Cruz.

We are exploring new territory. Matazlán on the Pacific coast of Mexico. It's an old port city on a picturesque peninsula with good beaches, shrimp fishing, minerals and fibres. This port call is a great, big work-up. Lots of delays. We are in *mañana* country again. Officials were late coming on board to clear the ship and it was a hassle to get the launches away. Eventually all passengers get ashore and I am on board all day preparing a thousand invitations for the Captain's Reception for Venezuelan embarks once we are through the Panama Canal.

If we got frustrated trying to get the ship cleared and passengers ashore it is nothing to the drama that developed later in the afternoon. A fierce wind has blown up and because of the squalls and high seas it is not safe to use the launches. So the passengers are stranded ashore waiting until the weather abates. Angry, tired, hungry. The novelty of a day in an unusual port quickly wears off when there is a hitch like this. Passengers want to be back on board, safe in the lap of luxury.

Getting passengers on and off launches is fraught with danger. A freak wave and the launch and gangway are an ocean apart. There are fully experienced members of the ship's company with strong, helping hands but it needs careful synchronisation for that important step out of the launch on to the gangway, both in perpetual motion with the sea. Many passengers are elderly, many wear spectacles. One false move and we can have a serious accident to deal with.

Cunard's number one priority is passenger safety. So a high swell means no chances are taken and passengers just have to wait until the weather improves and the launches can get them safely back on board. We had a lot of disgruntled passengers and many complaints about this unexpected delay but one thing we cannot control is the weather.

On to Acapulco and all is forgiven. High above the blue sea, overlooking the bay and hugging the natural contours of a flower-banked hillside, is the ultimate in luxury hotels, Las Brisas. It is built on the site of an old fortress – La Fortaleza San Carlos. The accommodation is a village of pink and white *casitas* – small houses – set on different levels on the hillside among the jacaranda trees and gardens full of flowers. Window walls open to a private swimming pool and verandah for each little house. Every day the swimming pool is cleaned and sprinkled with fresh hibiscus blossoms. When the sun goes down the pool is illuminated underwater for a moonlight dip.

A fleet of pink and white jeeps transports guests without cost whenever and wherever they want to go within the resort premises or down to the La Concha Beach Club – a private Club open to residents at this hotel, or to drive into Acapulco. No ties or jackets are required – dress is informal. Furs, jackets and ties are seldom seen in Acapulco, even in the evening. The atmosphere is that of a private club – there is no tipping.

A little further along this rocky cliff at a place called La Quebrada, a most remarkable feat takes place five times a day. One hundred and thirty feet below, the ocean crashes and fumes on to jagged rocks in a narrow chasm. Three young divers – *campeones clavadistas* – watch the incoming waves and judge exactly when to leap into the air. They take off like birds, seemingly not caring whether they live or die as they plunge into the waves and rocks below. Well... whatever turns you on... I feel cold to think of it. Close by there is a small shrine where they pray before leaping.

After Mexico we sailed for La Guaira, Venezuela. I was up at 5.30a.m. and wearing my hat, as instructed, made my way to the Bridge. This was it. Docking Day – D-Day – had arrived.

Pay attention and concentrate. I am introduced to the Pilot, a thick-set, middle-aged man, greying hair at the temples, still good-looking. I am told to stand near the echo-sounder. There is a hushed reverence on the Bridge, rather like being in a warm church. Captain Jones is leaning across the chart table, the Quartermaster is at the wheel, the Bridge Messenger is a couple of yards away from me and the Officer of the Watch scans the horizon. The Pilot prowls around the Bridge.

I keep still but my eyes follow everything and everybody. The mountains on the port side are breathtaking. Dark and brooding but the rising sun tints them, lightens them and then drenches them in gold as it bursts over the peaks. I can see a small plane landing on a strip near the beach. Slowly, very slowly we follow the narrow channel between two rows of marker buoys bobbing about in the sea.

The sharp-eyed Captain calls me to the table, shows me where we are and points to a symbol on the chart. The symbol indicates a marker buoy but the buoy cannot be seen out there in the water.

'Ask the Pilot what has happened to this buoy,' Captain Jones stabs the chart with his finger.

The Pilot shrugs his heavy shoulders, 'It was hit and sunk by a ship some weeks ago.'

No one had informed anyone but Captain Jones made a note and later dictated a letter to report it to Trinity House.

As we get closer we are surrounded by small vessels, fishing vessels, motor boats, yachts. We are in a nautical Piccadilly Circus. I get more and more nervous. Speed is very slow as we ease towards our allotted berth. The tugs are fussing around us, whistles are blowing. Orders are bouncing around the Bridge and every command is repeated and barked down to the Engine Room. There is total concentration. The atmosphere is electric.

By a superb team effort the 35,677 tons of the *Mauretania* comes safely alongside. In the fo'castle ropes are being thrown down to the stevedores who secure them round the bollards. The same is happening at the after end so that the *Mauretania* is captured, tricked, lured to a standstill. Gangways are placed and made secure. No more sailing the oceans for a while.

When passengers get to La Guaira they want to go to Caracas so the luxury coaches join the stream of traffic flowing on the super highway past the shacks and huts clinging to the hill sides. It slices through the mountains to Caracas nestling in a valley formed by branches of the coastal and the Andean mountain ranges.

My early morning start and frayed nerves on the Bridge responded to an extravagant breakfast – it felt like lunchtime anyway and I soon got my second wind. A gang of us hired a taxi and had the most wonderful day in Caracas. But at the back of my mind was the little demon grinning at me. Mocking me. I had to be on the Bridge at midnight for sailing... in the dark...

Caracas is a magnificent city of broad, leafy boulevards and squares, imposing equestrian statues and fine architecture with the Avila Mountain as a backdrop. Colour and music and flowers everywhere. A cable car takes tourists to the Humboldt Hotel at an altitude of 6,904 feet above sea level but all the passengers I spoke to were disappointed. The summit was shrouded in mist and they didn't see a thing.

Back on board and feeling refreshed after the stimulation of such sights and sounds I did not leave myself much time for the 'ordeal'. I couldn't get out of my cotton dress. It was low cut at the back and the zip fastener wouldn't move. The more I struggled the more I panicked. The zip would not slide and I couldn't see what the problem was. I went out into the corridor. Deserted. Not a Steward or Stewardess to be seen. The minutes were ticking away and I have to be there. On the Bridge. In uniform.

Grabbing a pair of nail scissors I walked along the corridor looking for someone, anyone who could cut me out of my dress. Eventually I came to a pantry where a Bedroom Steward was reading a newspaper. I told him my predicament. He stood behind me. I could feel his fingers probing and then he gave an almighty yank and the zip moved. And so did I!

Hot and flustered, my heart pounding, the adrenaline flowing, there I am standing on the Bridge again. Leaving La Guaira is spectacular in the dark. Lights flicker on the mountains, lights on motor boats and yachts bob about in the water, lights flash from headlights as cars whizz along the highway. The Bridge is in darkness with just the hum of the equipment and strangled voices on the crackling intercom. There is something about a ship's bridge at night. A sense of enormous power in that darkness.

I don't know what Navigators think about it but in my humble opinion it is easier in the dark. Like night-driving in a car, you can see the lights of the 'hazards', soon there are fewer and fewer. The mood seems to change perceptibly. Captain Jones and the Pilot wander to the wing of the Bridge. The *Maurie* is now clear of the flotsam and jetsam of the port and free to roam the oceans again.

I am dismissed and hurry to my cabin still on a high of adrenaline. I throw off my hat and shoes and deflate with sheer relief that it was all over and OK. Later, on thinking about my hours on the Bridge I wished I had known more about navigation, but that would need another lifetime and another career. At this time (the nineteen sixties) there were no female Captains in UK. Now there are, and it must be simply wonderful standing on that Bridge in total control guiding that massive feat of engineering in and out of narrow channels, battling with high winds at the entrance to harbours, riding the monstrous storms in the middle of the Atlantic. Yes, next time round I would like to be a Captain!

Back to reality and Lady Pursers – the atmosphere on board *Mauretania* for the Caribbean cruises was dynamic. We had an efficient, willing team with a great sense of humour in the Purser's Office. The pace was frantic but we always kept on top. The passengers had come to have a wonderful cruise and they did. They went ashore to visit the islands in the sunshine whilst New York was in the throes of a blizzard. Every voyage was full to capacity but every voyage we would have the sprinkling of moaners and complainers.

We had a notice board in the Purser's Office and it cannot be seen by passengers. It is festooned with bits of paper – the Port Duty Rota, Leave Rota, Safe Deposit Duty, Boat Drill Muster Stations and we had another list. It was our own special list headed '5-Star H.A.' And this is what it was about.

When a difficult passenger came to the counter and he/she gave us a hard time, whining and moaning and criticising, we put their name on this piece of paper with a star at the side of it. Well, the complainers always come again to complain about the same thing again, so they get another star. It was ever thus, ashore or afloat, complaining is a profession and some people are really expert at it. But if they get five stars they are awarded – The Five-star Horse's Arse. Of course, they knew nothing about this list or the honour we had bestowed upon them!

We had a full programme of entertainment and Carnival Night was a riot of fun and music and dancing. We had to encourage passengers to dress for this Carnival and longed to join in but we were not allowed to be out of uniform.

However, on the afternoon before Carnival Night, my shipmates dared me to dress up and go to the Main Lounge. Forbidden territory. All right! I owned a hideous black wig bought in Woolworths, New York. My stewardess got some bones from the Cook in the Galley. My good friends in the hairdressing salon, June and Heather, fixed my wig and coloured all the blonde bits of hair on my temples.

I wore a large black sombrero, a black mask with a black sweater, black leotards, a belt made of the bones, black court shoes (uniform) and I was in black from head to foot. My disguise was complete. I remember this night as if it happened yesterday! But it was nearly the end of my sea-going career.

Full of Bacardi and lime with back teeth awash I was painted and coloured and disguised beyond recognition and pushed down the back stairs and into the Main Lounge. It was humming. The dance floor was crowded and I was whisked away immediately. A certain

Purser, John Knight, danced with me but didn't recognise me. We worked side by side every day!

Then came the cabaret – Martha Graham and her world famous troupe of dancers. In for a penny, in for a pound – I was going to watch the cabaret too. It was standing room only and I joined the throng of passengers near the edge of the dance floor and was enjoying every moment of it when I felt a tap on my shoulder. Turning, I saw the Night Officer. He beckoned me to follow him out on to the covered Promenade Deck whereupon he whipped off my black sombrero, yanked off my black wig and there I was, looking and feeling a complete idiot!

'Get into uniform and report to the Staff Purser,' he barked pushing my wig and hat at me.

I did as I was told and went to find Ken Allen, Staff Purser.

The next morning Purser Bellamy sent for me (9.05a.m. according to my diary!) and accompanied me topsides to face Staff Captain Sheehan. This was it. I really thought I would be sacked and flown home from the next port.

'Yes,' I admitted, 'I was breaking rules by being out of uniform in the Main Lounge but the duty of the Purser's staff is to stimulate as much interest as possible for passengers to join in the 'theme' nights.' I knew I was speaking too quickly. 'And I was challenged to dress up and join in.'

There was a moment's silence and then Staff Captain Sheehan looked up from the papers on his desk and fixed me with a long, thoughtful stare. 'Don't do it again.' And that was the end of the affair.

My diary notes read 'Purser Bellamy was absolutely marvellous and supported me all the way.'

Now the Night Officer is a Navigating Officer doing the rounds of the bars and public rooms. How he found me in that mêlée I shall never know! So we can only assume that someone 'squealed' or he had picked up on it during his rounds and came looking for me.

Quite a number of people knew about the plans. The Cook in the galley provided the bones, girls in the Salon fixed my wig and tinted bits of my hair. There was a tremendous buzz around the ship. Always is on Carnival Night. I got caught but I didn't get sacked and I never did it again.

Cunard was exploring new commercial oceans in an effort to keep abreast of market trends. The *Queen Elizabeth* made her inaugural cruise to Nassau in the Bahamas in 1963 with 1309 passengers.

In 1965 the *Queen Mary* cruised for the first time to Las Palmas, Canary Islands.

'Inaugurals' were always a work-up. So many dignitaries, so many officials, so many journalists. But we needed good publicity for this new venture. Jack Frost of the *Daily Telegraph* and Montagu Lacey of the *Daily Express* travelled with us and gave glowing publicity. Jack Frost told me that he had sailed on the maiden voyage of the ship and never thought he would see such things

It was important that we sold the idea of cruising so we had to roll with the invasion from the press and public relations on shore. Everyone wanted to get on board to look at this famous liner.

After sailing we had thirty-six hours to check passports and type names on to manifests and balance the numbers. Here we go again! And we had thirty-six hours to write the envelopes for the invitations for every passenger to attend a cocktail party before arrival. Two parties before lunch, two parties before dinner and liqueur parties after dinner ensured that everyone would be invited to a cocktail party and entertained by ships' officers. It can be done!

But, listen to this. We are working behind closed shutters at the Purser's Office. It is 1a.m. The arrival documents and landing cards are all ready and a team of us are frantically scribbling the last names on the last envelopes for the cocktail parties. Down below in the Printer's Shop the cards are rolling off Big Bertha, a huge, noisy monster of a printing machine. Grey with fatigue the Printer arrives at the office with stacks and stacks of the invitation cards. We all grab a pile and start to stuff the envelopes. But the cards don't fit. They're too big!!

You could have scraped us from the bulkheads!

A good bit of lateral thinking by the Printer. He scoops them up and takes them back to the Printer's Shop and slices them down to the size of the envelope. It meant sabotaging the crinkly gold edge of the invitation card and passengers, none the wiser, got a plain white one. Mission accomplished with a great deal of team work. I have a note in my diary that we got to bed at 3.30a.m. Up at 5a.m. for docking at 6a.m.

When we were cruising we had more social duties. Every night at sea was a theme night. Fancy Dress, Caribbean Carnival, Twenties Night, Red and Gold Ball, Neapolitan Night, Ladies Night, Black and White Ball, Fiesta Night, Krazy Nite, Irish Night, Get Together Night and Farewell Night – you name it, we did it...

We encouraged passengers to dress up in the appropriate garb to make that particular night a success. They were very responsive and readily entered into the fun. And there was nothing like a good cocktail party to get them in the mood!

We also had daytime events. Our English Country Fair was always successful. I had a stall 'Guess the weight of the Social Director.' The charge was 25 cents for one guess and we raised $48 pondering over the weight of Bryan, Social Director – a Harry Secombe look alike. In fact, Sir Harry was in the suite of rooms next to our office and we could hear him practising in the mornings. And he would often pop into the office and on one occasion suggested that he and Bryan would make a good pair of bookends!

The *Mauretania* cruising season was rounded off with a Mediterranean cruise but the weather that Spring was disappointing. We anchored at Gibraltar at 7a.m. It was dark when I went to the office so I didn't see the famous rock until later in the day. Looking across the Straits of Gibraltar I could see Tangier thirty miles away.

I had two hours off at Tangier and headed for the Kasbah just a short distance from the dock. Bumped into some of the Cruise Staff who wouldn't let me go to the Kasbah on my own. We walked under a domed archway into a warren of steep, narrow streets riddled with alleyways.

The place was teeming with people, barefoot children, dogs, cats, goats. Beggars at every corner. Shops and bazaars with all their goods arranged at the doorway and it stank to high heaven of dogs, cats, goats and stale tobacco. At every turn we were invited to 'buy good things very cheap'.

Sicily was bitterly cold. We had a hailstorm. The town of Messina is surrounded by high snow-capped mountains with Mount Etna in the distance. Passengers were able to make a tour overland from Messina to rejoin the ship at Catania in the afternoon but the weather was so bad that the launch service from ship to shore was suspended and we had about five hundred cold, wet and hungry passengers stranded in Catania for more than two hours until the weather abated. We eventually got everyone back on board and sailed for Malta.

The bad weather persisted and we were unable to enter Valetta harbour because of high winds and heavy swell so we went on to Piraeus. The 'off-duties' took the local train to Athens. From the rocky heights of the Acropolis we could see the Chapel of St George, the Parthenon, the Tower of the Winds, the Temple of Jupiter and – my favourite – the Caryatids at the Erechtheum – the Temple of the Wingless Victory. This is a group of beautifully sculpted young maidens, Caryatids, supporting the porch. The maidens came from a Greek village outside Athens and performed an unusual dance ending with the right toe poised on the ground. They are dressed in flowing robes which adhere to the body as though wet. One of these figures was removed and replaced by a substitute of Portland cement. It is easily recognisable. The original is in England. Greece has not forgiven Lord Elgin for this theft and others he committed. But now all the glories of ancient Greece are threatened by the dirt and dust and erosion and traffic fumes.

I sat in one of the marble seats at the Theatre of Dionysus and was surprised how comfortable it was. They are well shaped and have arm rests. The guide told us that the dignitaries and priests always sat in the same place and in fact their name and date is on the seat. When the Romans came to Greece they made modifications to the theatre including the laying of a marble floor for the stage. The original floor was earth because the actors wore wooden-soled shoes and could move about silently without drowning words or music.

We drove to Cape Sunion and the Temple of Poseidon where I saw Lord Byron's name engraved on a pilaster. It is not the only name – Louis Ravel, G. L. A. Scott, J. Rodger, H. M. Warren and others have left their mark. I have no idea who they are but assume they were on their Grand Tour when they indulged in this tourist vandalism. We visited the Temple of Corinth where St Paul delivered his address to the Corinthians. In fact, we gorged on a feast of cultural history.

We had four whole days in Cairo, two on duty, two off. Here we ran into all kinds of delays. A convoy of ships was coming through the Suez Canal and we were unable to enter the harbour until they were clear. And we had difficulties with our manifests. Additional copies were demanded – here we go again. One Assistant Purser slipped a Littlewood's Football Coupon into the pile of manifests to be approved by the Egyptian authorities. It got the official Immigration stamp without question!

I joined the Crew Excursion to Cairo. We drove across the Nile Delta through primitive villages, just squalid little huddles of wooden shacks. Children played in the dirt and dust and at the doorway of one shack I saw two girls squatting on their haunches, one picking through the other one's head, presumably for lice.

The desert either side of the road was soon replaced by fertile green land. Most farms had buffalo to draw a wooden plough with just one plough share on which stood a man, woman or child to give more weight to bite into the land. The women working in the fields looked as if they were picking potatoes. The men and women were dressed in full length gowns of black, grey or striped cotton. The women were veiled and the men wore what looked like a turban. Time stood still and we could have been gazing at a Biblical scene.

There were camels laden with goods ambling along the fields. There were donkeys and mules weighed down with vegetables and bundles. At intervals the coach was halted by police at check points – we had ten between Port Said and Cairo! We saw the Nile, very muddy and very calm.

The camels at Giza were bedecked with coloured rugs and pompoms on the saddles and seemed very disgruntled. They make a peculiar noise, a mixture of a child's squeal and donkey's bray, and who can blame them with so much genuflecting in the sand! Every other minute someone is climbing on or off their backs.

We scrambled around the pyramids and succumbed to the offer of a dragoman with a leathery face and no teeth. He gave us a cavernous grin and took us to the foot of the largest one (Cheops), 466 feet high and covering 13 acres – a masterpiece of technical skill and engineering. We went into a narrow tunnel which slanted downwards. In front of us was a long wooden ladder, just an ordinary ladder like the ones we used to climb the haystacks at home.

We started to climb step by step, inside the pyramid. Every now and again we arrived at a small platform where we could straighten our backs then up we went again, higher and higher on this creaky ladder until we stepped into a large square room. The guide told us we were about half way up the pyramid and were in The King's Chamber. It was bare except for an empty, lidless sarcophagus without any inscription or ornament.

The descent was more perilous – I was in high heels (I was young and stupid!) and coming down those steep steps was quite an ordeal. The guide insisted on going first – that is, he was below me. I was wearing a dress and kept my eyes glued to the rungs of this rickety ladder. He kept his eyes on me – or my little white knickers – until we got down. Serves me right.

On to the crumbling Sphinx just a short distance away, and then back to Cairo along straight dusty roads punctuated with telegraph poles. We passed a mule, its owner astride the bundles of produce. Otherwise the road was deserted.

The Citadel commands a wonderful view over Cairo. From the battlements I saw mosques and minarets, a maze of streets and back alleyways and in the distance – sand, sand and more sand.

At the Mosque of Mohammed Ali we were asked to put covers over our shoes before entering. The mosque was breathtaking. Cut glass chandeliers sparkled in the light of hundreds and hundreds of candles.

We drove back through Port Ismailia, once an important British garrison town and now deserted, much to the residents' sorrow. Many of our ship's company had served in the Armed Forces and knew Ismailia so it was quite a nostalgic visit for them.

And back on board, dirty, smelly, tired and happy. There was so much to remember. The ancient culture, the rituals, the wonders of the world. And so much to forget – the squalor, the poverty. It all piles up, port after port, country after country until I get geographical indigestion and it's difficult to relate the sights, sounds and cultures to the correct places. But I have to keep gorging. Writing notes, diaries and letters and taking photos helps to sort it all out.

There is no let up – on to Haifa in Israel nestling on the slopes of Mount Carmel about one hundred and fifty miles up the coast from Egypt. We always visited Egypt first because Israeli Immigration stamps in a passport were not acceptable in Egypt. We had a two-day visit. I was off duty on the second day and the Senior First Navigating Officer had the Captain's limousine, a Cadillac, at his disposal – would I care to join him and other officers for the day? Our chauffeur was Aaron, speaking immaculate English.

We saw large modern chemical and paint factories. Everywhere was spotlessly clean and there were no beggars. We drove to Nazareth. Aaron first took us to Mary's Grotto. He led us down some dark, stone steps to what is now a shrine. There was an altar, lit by candles, the floor was marble and there was a beautiful painting of Mary on one wall. The guide told us that 'the Angel Gabriel appeared unto Mary in this cave and told her that she would bear a son'. Standing there surrounded by a crowd of tourists it was difficult to absorb. I felt we had no business there – or had we?

We were then led along the street to St Joseph's Church. This was built above the cave where Joseph and Mary lived and brought up Jesus. At the rear of the church we went down stone steps into a room with an altar and marble floor. This was where Joseph worked as a carpenter repairing plough shares and other wooden farm implements then we go down yet more narrow stone steps into a cave, rather like an igloo. There was a hole in the centre of the ceiling where light came through from the church above but when it was occupied by the Holy Family the light would have been from the sky above. We were told that 'Joseph, Mary and Jesus lived, ate and slept in this cave and it was their home until Jesus was 27 years of age'.

We decided to have lunch at Tiberias on the shores of the Sea of Galilee. It is a beautiful lake in a bowl of mountains. Thirteen miles long, seven miles wide it was bigger than I imagined. The mountain range bordering the opposite side of the lake was the Golan Heights.

We are sitting at a table, al fresco, gazing across this legendary sea when from the corner of my eye a man with a beard wearing a long beige robe is edging towards our table. He's clutching a bundle of cards.

The Senior First beckons him closer. 'What have you got there?'

The man with the beard grins. He has badly-stained teeth leaning into his mouth. He sidles up to the others, fanning through the postcards. Then he points to me.

I reach for the postcards but he steps back pressing the cards close to his chest, then he throws his arms wide.

'You sell missy to me,' he grins those teeth at us again. 'For postcards. Very good. No?'

One of our fellows nods agreement and flicks through the cards.

'Six dutty postcards. For missy. Yes.'

The Senior First slowly eases his six foot frame from the chair and points at nothing in particular. 'Bugger off!'

And the vendor was gone. No sale!

From Tiberias we drove to a church on the hillside in the village of Tabgha. The interior of this church was simplicity itself. There was a table where the altar would have been and beneath this table was a mosaic of a basket of loaves flanked by fish. We were told that it was at this place that Christ performed the miracle of the loaves and fishes. The floor was a splendid mosaic of birds, fishes, beasts and flowers of this lake region.

Further along the northern shore of the Sea of Galilee we visited the ruins of the village of Capernaum. Christ made this village the centre of his activities for about two years and many of His miracles were performed here. Saul was born here. Today Capernaum is no more than a heap of ruins in the midst of palm trees beside the lake shore. Lying all around on the ground are pieces of rock, jars and pots said to have been used by the villagers. I was surprised they had not been stolen but security was tight.

From Capernaum we climbed high across the mountains and looked down on the River Jordan. We drove down through hilly, rocky country to the city of Acre where Richard the Lionheart lost his fortress in 1291. It was getting dark and there was not a soul to be seen as we wandered through the old walled city. I have a graphic recollection of strolling under the arches and along the sombre passages of this deserted fortress to peer down on the sullen waters of the Mediterranean swirling below.

It was a starry night with a thin moon watching over the battlements. These ruins are the only remains of the long stirring history of Acre which had 17 recorded sieges. The crusaders have gone. The battles are over. It was eerie and ghostly. Time stood still echoing something brooding and sinister, dark and powerful. Memories of Acre are deeply scored in my memory.

When we docked at Haifa the following year a group of us went to Bethlehem. The entrance to the Church of the Nativity was low and narrow to prevent marauders from entering the church with their horses. The facade originally had three doors – two of them were walled up. Once again we went down to a cave. A silver star with Latin inscription marks the spot where Christ was born. The walls of the Grotto are covered with asbestos guaranteed against fire, donated in 1874 by MacMahon, President of the French Republic.

The manger lies to the right of the spot where Jesus was born and was probably used for storing fodder. This rectangular cave area is very small, (35 feet by 10 feet) lit by candles and seems crowded although only a few tourists at a time are allowed to enter. Once again I felt we were rubbernecking. It would have been wonderful to stand alone, to see and sense the occasion but of course, that was out of the question.

Jerusalem is five miles north of Bethlehem and is very, very crowded but the via Dolorosa is probably much the same as it was in the days of Christ. Narrow, crowded alleyways and steps winding and weaving past bazaars, street vendors, beggars and mules, to the last five stations located within the Church of the Holy Sepulchre standing over Golgotha, the place of the Crucifixion and the tomb where the body of Jesus was laid.

In spite of all those tourists, fidgeting with cameras, brochures, water bottles and whatever else was bothering them, the low buzz of voices, the coughs, and the irritating noises of my fellow tourists I felt quite emotional.

The Wailing Wall is a sheer sandy-coloured wall of considerable height. Men stand facing it. Women stand in a similar fashion at the same wall a short distance away. Known as the Western Wall it is the portion that Herod built around the second Temple in 20 BC. Tourists watch from a spacious esplanade.

We stopped on a well-made tarmac road looking across to the Garden of Gethsemane with its ancient olive trees. It is said that the age of eight of these trees is lost in antiquity. Some Botanists claim that they are Roman olive trees and may be 3000 years old! We were told that this Garden at the foot of the Mount of Olives appears today as it was twenty centuries ago.

Most of the churches we saw have been modified and rebuilt, reconstructed and restored over the centuries but I thought this famous garden was quite beautiful and timeless and natural.

It all rather took my breath away – to be gazing at these scenes, to know that beneath my feet, during 4000 years of recorded history, more wars have been fought here than in any other city in the world. There is a sense of wonder. The land cannot be separated from what took place here. It was awesome.

But it's time to go back on board, back to the passports and landing cards, the cocktail parties and whoopsy-do nights for the passengers. Just in case it's beginning to sound like one long holiday, remember we are preparing documents for each of these ports and dealing with countless passenger problems such as lost passports, stolen wallets, accidents, illnesses and deaths often in difficult weather conditions. There is a note in my diary here: 'Very, very tired of people. It is an effort to be polite.' But I am more than thrilled to take advantage of the optional extras that come with the job.

When we docked at Southampton a new challenge was waiting for me.

It's the *QE2*

But something was happening. The mighty *Queens* were like ghost ships. We were not getting the bookings and we did not hear the roar of the jet airliners in the skies high above us any more than we got the message in that cocktail party given by American Airlines at the Waldorf Astoria, drinking champagne and eating canapés and celebrating the new 'jet service'. Our passengers were flying across the Atlantic in a matter of hours. The *Queens* took five days!

Cunard sent out a memorandum about the reorganisation of the passenger fleet. Both *Queens* were trading at an annual loss. *Queen Mary* was to be withdrawn and *Queen Elizabeth* would be run as a profitable unit, cruising in the winter months and operating the transatlantic summer service. Staff would be reduced by 1,000. A mini-earthquake rumbled through the ships.

Cunard had already entered the fly/cruise market with the *Sylvania* and plans for the new, modern design of Q4 had gone beyond the drawing board. She would have lower operating costs and would be able to go through Suez and Panama Canals which neither *Queen* could do. They were restricted in their ports of call by their size and they were at the end of their working lives – the end of an era.

Q4 was the designation used by the shipyard to refer to *Queen Elizabeth 2*. She was the fourth Queen liner to be planned but No. 3 was never built.

Q4 would be versatile for both North Atlantic passengers and cruising which was predicted to be the leisure pastime for the future. How right they were!

Queen Elizabeth 2 made her debut in a blaze of glory on 20th September 1967. Sleek and slim with only one funnel that looked rather like a penny whistle! We were glued to the television screen in Cunard's office in Southampton as she sliced into the River Clyde and into our sensibilities. She was 66,851 tons. Much smaller than the old *Queens* but she had fifty per cent more passenger space because of the modern lightweight materials used in her construction. She cost £30 million and she could carry 1815 passengers and crew of 1000.

The tonnage has increased over the years due to the addition of penthouse suites.

President Tito of Yugoslavia attributed his survival to his ability to change with the times. Well, Cunard changed with the times and survived. Departments were restructured. Pursers became Hotel Officers so did Catering Officers, all in the new Hotel Department which combined Pursers and Catering. I was recycled and came out as Social Secretary but more about that later. There was such an outcry from passengers when they realised that there was no Purser on board that the title was quickly reinstated. Masters at Arms became Security Officers.

And the ship – so different. It bore no comparison with the old *Queens*. They were like stately country homes with their sweeping staircases, their hushed lounges, their panelled staterooms. There was no public address system. Bellboys carried messages around the ship but now everyone knows what's going on all the time.

The *Queen Elizabeth 2* was such a kaleidoscope of colour. The Midships Lobby – the first place the passenger saw when embarking – was circular with emerald green leather seat benches, chrome trim and dark carpet.

The Queen's Room had cream curtains and a cream carpet flecked with burnt orange. Chairs like oyster shells. It was all so light and so refined.

The Double Down Room was furnished in shades of red, mauve, purple, cerise. A spiral staircase led up to the shopping gallery.

The Midships Bar lounge had a black carpet, black velvet walls, small, circular glass-topped tables. The ceiling was entirely in gold leaf. This was a most stylish venue for the ladies in their gorgeous evening gowns and jewels glinting against the dark velvet walls and gold ceiling. It took our breath away.

Here was an exciting, modern liner beyond the imagination.

Over the years there has been much refurbishing of public rooms and the decor has changed several times. Go with the flow!

My 80-day week

After the departure of both *Queens* from the ocean scene I was invited to serve in *Queen Elizabeth 2*. This time with a different task and a different title. Cunard's Executive in Southampton presented the job specification to me. I would be signed on as Social Secretary for the

Queen Elizabeth 2 World Cruises and I was – quote – to mastermind all the invitations to the Captain's official Receptions and Farewells held at every port and to organise the private cocktail parties given by passengers – unquote.

The fundamental reason for this new position was explained to me. The cocktail invitation for the Captain's official parties had been an item in the Daily Programme delivered to rooms (new name for cabin) every morning. But some passengers did not read the Daily Programme. And some passengers were of the opinion that after paying eighty thousand pounds for a cruise he/she should not be invited to cocktails with the Captain via a paragraph in the Daily Programme. Quite right, too.

There would be a Social Director, Bryan Vickers, a Purser with whom I had sailed many times. A man of the utmost integrity, with a spontaneous smile, a wicked sense of humour and not a mean thought in his head. I accepted.

In addition, the Company had engaged supplementary staff – a group of ten Americans. Mature, well-dressed, well-educated men, former executive officers or ex-military personnel. I called them The Terrible Ten – they were great. Always willing to help in my sphere of operation when needed. But primarily they were there to listen to the ladies travelling alone, to chat, to dance, to assist on the shore excursions or whatever. On one World Cruise I had more than six hundred unaccompanied ladies wanting to dance and enjoy themselves – we could have done with a hundred of those men.

The *Queen Elizabeth 2* left Southampton for New York mid-December to make Christmas and New Year cruises. In early January Bryan and I were instructed to fly to Nassau to join the ship at her last port before New York so that we could get our office up and running before sailing round the world.

Our instructions were to arrive Nassau 8p.m. and join *QE2* sailing at 11p.m. When we got to the quayside we couldn't believe our eyes. *Queen Elizabeth 2* was disappearing into the deep, dark blue beyond, a myriad of lights in the darkness as she steamed into the night! *HELP!*

Bryan knew exactly what to do. We wheeled into the Port Authority office on the dock and woke up a man in a woolly hat.

'Do you have a ship to shore telephone?' Bryan bristled with efficiency.

The man rubbed his eyes, yawned, gave us both a once over and took us into a small office. Bryan called up the Bridge of the *QE2* and reported our 'position'. Stranded on the dock at Nassau. The Staff Captain answered. Believe it or not. The largest liner in the world would wait for us if we got a launch out to the ship straight away.

By now the Port Agent had picked up our call on his walkie-talkie and came to us in the Port Authority office. He knew a man with a launch, a former Captain. He had lost his Master's ticket when he put his ship on the rocks off the Scilly Isles! He willingly agreed to take us out to the *QE2*. Eight pieces of baggage, a drunken AB, (able-bodied Seaman) two unknown Bahamians, me and Bryan stepped into the launch and set off across the moonlit harbour towards the starburst of lights in the distance.

The launch was painfully slow and the lights of the *QE2* seemed to slip further and further away from us. As we approached someone was signalling with an Aldis lamp from the port side of the Bridge. The owner of the launch, the former Captain, could not read Morse. But Bryan could! He is ex-RAF air crew (Lancaster bombers) and he read the message. We were to go forward to Port side shell doors.

In all my years at sea I have never boarded a ship by rope ladder. I had watched pilots do it many times but there I was standing in the launch as it bobbed about like a cork, staring up at a sheer black cliff face. The drunken sailor was sent up first, then it was my turn. I kicked off my shoes and stuffed them into my flight bag then I was strapped into a harness. Then with both hands I grabbed the rope either side of the small wooden ladder and began to climb keeping my eyes focussed on the black metal wall in front of my nose.

After sitting in a plane for twelve hours there wasn't much left in my batteries and I was amazed at the lack of strength in my arms. I couldn't get any purchase. The rope ladder seemed too flimsy and too flexible. There was nothing firm or solid about it and my arms seemed to be made of elastic – they stretched away and I found it difficult to hoist myself. It was a long way up but I stayed calm and concentrated. Then I got to the opening and numerous strong arms were reaching out for me and I stepped into the shell doors. Bryan arrived at my side in no time, then the luggage was brought up on ropes.

There was a message waiting for us. We were to report to the Captain immediately. I thought it was for a dressing down, detaining a ship full of cruise passengers – but it wasn't our fault. Southampton Office told us to join *QE2* sailing from Nassau 11p.m. Sailing time had been changed to 7p.m. a week earlier but no one had told us!

However, I didn't get told off. We both got a big welcome from Captain Doug Ridley and Staff Captain Alan Bennell. We were offered brandy and steak sandwiches – in that order. And that was the second finest hour of my sea-going career. Confidence builds with these unexpected escapades.

Recently on a cargo ship the Chief Officer invited me to join him and the Carpenter on Hold Inspection at eight o'clock in the morning. Wear trousers and trainers. The industrial gloves he gave me were very cumbersome. This time I was going down sheer metal ladders into the bowels of a ship at sea without harness or hard hat off the coast of Peru. It was like storming a cathedral! But that story must wait.

We had a luxurious office on Boat Deck. It was an expensive suite room so why wasn't it sold to passengers at eighty thousand pounds a cruise? We were immediately above the Theatre Bar which was a discotheque at night and throbbing until dawn. No one could possibly have slept in that room. That's why we came to have a super office on Boat Deck with panoramic sea views.

It had an ankle-deep cream carpet flecked with rust. Two desks, floral arrangements, good cupboard space, one of which was converted to a bar. Most evenings at sea the office was transformed by the stewards so that we could entertain a group of passengers to cocktails. The two desks were pushed to the wall, covered with a white damask tablecloth, adorned with flowers and greenery and we were ready to welcome twenty people. When I got to the office next morning everything was functional again as a busy centre for organising parties and dealing with passenger problems.

The Captain, Hotel Manager and other Senior Officers entertained a group of passengers each evening at sea. These invitations were dealt with by the Captain's Secretary, Lynn Waring, and we worked closely to co-ordinate guest lists and avoid duplications. We had to go through the entire passenger list of about one thousand five hundred passengers.

Every passenger was invited to a Captain's Reception after embarking and every passenger was invited to a Captain's Farewell before disembarking. I was responsible for the administration involved with these marathon guest lists – about six or seven hundred invitations for a Reception or Farewell – and for the private parties given by the passengers, as many as two hundred guests at eight or nine different venues every evening.

The Captain's Reception was held the night after sailing which gave just a matter of hours to personally address these envelopes. An impossible task for one mortal! But help was at hand. The Terrible Ten rallied round before going on their evening duties. Those with the best handwriting joined in the scribble. Others sorted the envelopes by deck, port and starboard, ready for delivery. So almost before the passengers had unpacked they received an invitation to cocktails with the Captain.

Late bookings and errors on the manifest and room changes were a big concern but if anyone was missed they would get an invitation for another evening.

It was my responsibility to order sufficient cards and envelopes for the eighty-day cruise. We used thousands of them but if we ran out of cards or envelopes halfway across the Pacific Ocean I was out of business. So I had my head in a wet towel for a week before leaving Southampton, estimating and budgeting stationery requirements.

Some passengers booking private parties asked for their invitations to be printed on board and invariably gave me their guest list so in addition to the official parties, I prepared the envelopes and invitation cards and typed lists for the private parties, too.

This was a simple enough task so long as the writing was legible, but some of these party ideas were given life in the early hours of the morning in one of the night clubs or bars with guests' names scribbled on a serviette or the back of an envelope or a cocktail tariff card. But our motto in the office was 'It can be done'.

My great ally was the Chief Printer, Roy Rundell – a shipmate from *Mauretania* days. Often the passenger wanted extra cards to be printed at short notice or cocktail invitations in Spanish, French or German. A big work-up on top of the mountain of print jobs turned out by him and his team. Daily programmes, daily newspaper, menus, log cards. The Printer's shop was hot and noisy and way down below in the bowels of the ship but he always produced for me.

After departure from New York I would be inundated with bookings for private parties. Within an hour of sailing I had taken bookings for 2,400 people to go to private cocktail parties.

There were seven, and at a push, eight locations in the ship that could be used for these private parties. The 'push' came when all venues were fully booked and the pressure was on to find space for another party. Those of you who know the *QE2* will recall the very elegant Queen's Room. So chic. So sophisticated. Athwartships, in a recess, is a magnificent sculpture of the head and shoulders of Her Majesty Queen Elizabeth II. This venue was code-named *UHMB*. (Under Her Majesty's Bust) The Queen's Room was for general passenger use but this special area was my saviour when I was being shredded and put through the wringer because all venues had been booked.

The most sought-after location was the Princess Grill Lounge similar to the Midships Bar Lounge. It is small. It is intimate. Maximum number of guests, twenty. Just inside the door on the right in a small alcove is a miniature water garden with greenery and exotic plants discreetly illuminated – all done with mirrors very effectively.

The Lounge walls are deep purple velvet, benches in dark crimson and chrome-edged tables on a thick purple-black carpet creating a marvellous back-drop for the ladies in their fabulous gowns and brilliant jewels. Pause on the short flight of stairs that leads up to the Princess Grill and look down on the scene in that small Lounge. It was pure glamour.

During my first World Cruise a passenger was giving a party on arrival in Singapore. She wanted purple flowers to match her dress, her amethysts and the decor in the Princess Grill Lounge. I cabled the Agent for the flowers but when they arrived on board they were absolutely useless. Limp and dangly and looking so sorry for themselves. They could not be revived. So no purple flowers for the party. That was the first and last time I ordered flowers for a passenger. The following year we had a flower shop on board. The florist knew exactly how to cosset the unusual flowers in all temperatures and the shipboard flower shop was a great financial success.

Every evening these eight rooms were booked for private parties and every evening they had to be prepared by the stewards just as the host or hostess wished. A certain number of chairs and tables and the lighting had to be just so. These passengers were connoisseurs at party-throwing and I remember spending the entire morning with one lady in a penthouse suite discussing her requirements. She remarked quite casually that the last party she gave was in the Hollywood Bowl!

I was kept very busy with these bookings and often there was a queue of passengers waiting to book a party. I would ask them to take a seat in the Double Down Room as they all wished to discuss their plans in privacy. But all the parties on board, official and private, were a tremendous success. Passengers had come to enjoy themselves and they did.

The passengers were very discriminating and knew exactly what they wanted – almost to the measurement of the hors d'oeuvres. Sometimes I would be handed a recipe for a sauce or a dip to send to the Chef to make up! Another passenger complained that the caviar served on a small, round biscuit made the biscuit soggy. Could it be served on a square (2 inch) of Melba toast? Certainly, Madam.

I then completed a form for every Private Cocktail Party, listing all requirements.

'Mixed drinks, Bar set up, crayfish (v. cold) on toothpicks with red dip and dilled mayonnaise with cucumber dip. Melon pieces with prosciutto ham (no fat) bite size. Flowers, (Antherium – red and white with fern). 20 guests.'

And that's just one party order! Here's another –

'Mixed drinks, cold canapés, Mexican corn chips, Avocado dip with grated onion (Guacamole), Cream cheese dip with celery salt, soya sauce. 45 guests. 'Tommy' to be incuded in Bar staff.'

This form was then photo-copied and sent to the Ship's Controller; Food & Beverage Manager; Administration; Executive Chef; Cruise Director; Public Room Officer; Captain's Secretary; Chief Barkeeper; Chief Deck Steward; Photographers and Public Room Supervisor. So there was no excuse for anyone not knowing what was going on!

There was great rivalry among the passengers giving parties. I would be asked what Mrs So and So had ordered for her party, or which wine or champagne was served at Mr So and So's party. I always replied that I didn't have the records. It was a fib. All records were kept for the entire cruise and passengers' requests were dealt with in total confidence but they often tried to outdo each other.

The request that made me want to hide in a cupboard was for a pianist or trio to play during the cocktail party! The musicians worked late hours and were not keen to be dragged out of bed to play so early in the evening. There was a piano to move (!) there were the overtime rules, hours of rest and so on... It was all very complicated.

The desire for party-giving was so intense that I had a waiting list for room cancellations. Sometimes large denomination dollar bills were passed across my desk to effect a booking. I would slide the money back again explaining as tactfully and diplomatically as possible that such an action was not necessary. I was retained by Cunard and should there be a cancellation I would make contact immediately. I had eighty action-packed days of work to get through – I didn't need bribery!

After the party the passenger was billed for the food and drink consumed. They were surprised that we didn't charge for the use of the room. More than 300 private parties were held during a World Cruise and more than 14,000 invitations were sent out. I don't think anyone realised at the time just what an enormous attraction the private cocktail parties would be – I certainly did not expect such a deluge and it was a good revenue earner for Cunard.

Sometimes we travelled west through the Panama Canal and across the Pacific Ocean. Sometimes we travelled south through the Caribbean and down to Rio de Janeiro then east across the South Atlantic to South Africa. And we were sailing through different time zones which meant that the ship's clocks were always being advanced or retarded.

Los Angeles was often our first American landfall at the end of the cruise. This meant a Captain's Farewell Party for as many as eight hundred passengers disembarking and then – wait for it – we would embark nine hundred passengers to travel coastwise with us, through the Panama Canal to Port Everglades and New York. And yes, we started all over again with cocktail invitations for these passengers to attend a Captain's Reception.

I was just about ready to be carried home in a basket after eighty days of whoopsy-doo. But there was no let up. So – smile and –

'Welcome aboard! How nice to see you.'

I've never been ashore in Los Angeles.

I had to attend all the Captain's Reception and Farewell parties and almost without exception, the host or hostess of the private parties expected me to attend their party. I got it down to a fine art. I couldn't attend one and not another. You may wonder how I stayed sober. Well, I quickly learned how to pace myself and developed a getaway strategy. It was quite easy to take one sip and after a few minutes of mixing and mingling leave the glass of champagne on a table. No one was going to check! And in this way I could do the rounds with a few sips and a clear head. I never acquired a taste for whisky or gin, only the product of the grape. I know many of the Captains would be clutching a glass of what appeared to be gin and tonic. They were, in fact, drinking tonic water with ice and lemon!

Another trick we learned was to keep the glass in the right hand. After shaking more than seven hundred hands and mixing and mingling with the guests immediately there was no possibility to get away to wash hands. Always take canapés with the left hand. But I did not escape. The skin on the knuckles of my right hand is badly disfigured – according to my Dermatologist there is no cure! No wonder the Queen wears gloves!

So I was in at the deep end again and it was a far cry from checking passports and visas and balancing manifests and passenger stenography. And I had a lot to learn. The ship was 'colour-coded'. Different colours for different decks which were numbered one to five, not lettered as in the old *Queens* (Prom. Main, A, B, C.) Unlike the *Caronia*, who embarked passengers in New York and kept them all to bring back to New York, the *QE2* had wayport passengers. The world cruises were sold in segments and passengers were embarking and disembarking at most ports, so a Captain's Reception and Captain's Farewell every time.

With these segment cruises the scene was ever changing, especially when we got to the Far East. The young passengers brought a brilliant splash of colour to all our events. Their salaries must have been mega-yen to afford such a wardrobe of designer clothes.

And of course there was the unusual, the unexpected, the bizarre. En route to Acapulco a retired Admiral asked us to arrange a wedding reception on board. He planned to marry a passenger in Acapulco. Arrangements were in full swing when a few hours later the wedding was called off. Engagements and weddings were *de rigueur* on a world cruise.

One of my worst nightmares when booking the parties was the International Date Line. Two days with the same date. Did Madam want Tuesday No. 1 or Tuesday No. 2 for her party? After a late night and a hangover passengers were totally confused. Where are we – Tuesday No. 1 or Tuesday No. 2? They were all at sea, literally, over the Date Line. And in the swimming pool if they were not careful.

I was initiated into this Crossing the Line ceremony during my *Mauretania* days. Buckets of shaving cream and gallons of rum come to mind. Or perhaps it was the other way round! One initiation was enough for me. I kept out of the way on the *QE2*!

Sometimes the Captain would pay us a visit at midday so we would close the office, open the bar and have our own little party for Crossing the Line!

Land Ahoy

Land below the Wind

So, we're on our way around the world. I'm not going to tell you about all the ports we visited. Too boring and you've probably been there, done that and got the T-shirt. I'm going to tell you about my adventures and some of the places that impressed me most.

Let's go! Sabah, East Malaysia occupying the northern part of Borneo in the South China Sea. The Land below the wind. 'Borneo' was not unfamiliar to me and I'll tell you why. As I said earlier, my sisters and I spent hours playing in the fields and woods and streams at that lonely farm and we'd come in for tea looking as if we'd been pulled through a hedge backwards. Mother would say, 'Gracious me, you look like the wild women from Borneo.'

Never in my most fanciful daydream could I have ever believed that I would visit that country. But here we are approaching the dockside at Kota Kinabalu, formerly Jesselton. It was a British Protectorate until 1888. The country gained independence in 1963.

Time ashore depends on my workload so it is up to me to get organised. I did not think there would be many passengers embarking at Kota Kinabalu, therefore no Captain's Reception, so before leaving New York I wrote to our Landing Agent in Kota Kinabalu asking him to hire a jeep or Land-Rover with local driver for the day. I want to explore on my own but as I reread the research notes I'd made before leaving home, I am having doubts. The country is so remote, I do not speak their language and I could disappear without trace in those mountains.

So I invite a passenger to come with me. A young South African, travelling alone. Doctor Carlos de Nobrega. He jumps at the idea. I told him what to expect. A jeep and driver. Sand flies near the rivers and mosquitoes everywhere. Snakes, but I was confident that he would know what to do about a snake bite. Rough, jungle tracks infested with leeches. I told him I had a box of matches and would bring them. Strike a match, apply to its bum and it will soon let go!

But there was a big problem. And a serious one. South African passports were vetoed all around the world at that time (1980) and many Immigration authorities refused to allow South Africans to land but thanks to Bryan Vickers, the Social Director, we got around the difficulty. Carlos was issued with a crew landing card and came ashore with me on the staff launch.

The Landing Agent told us to go to the Tourist Office just a short walk in the shade of lush trees and shrubs and there, sure enough, we find the Land-Rover complete with driver, Henry, late thirties perhaps, stockily built, medium height, unsmiling. In fact he is rather taciturn, a bit wary perhaps but it *is* early in the morning. So off we go with Henry, spare petrol and water.

I have set my mind on getting to the foothills of Mount Kinabalu, 14,000 ft. It is still rising – one estimate is 5mm per year – and the landslides on its slopes and rock debris beneath its peaks are evidence of the continuing erosion.

Traffic is heavy and it takes some time to get clear of this modern city, with clusters of white multi-storey shops, offices and flats, tree-lined streets, all clean and tidy. New buildings are going up everywhere and earth-moving vehicles and trucks block the road.

Soon we are passing huts on stilts, water lilies growing in swampy fields by the side of the road, water buffalo wallowing in the mud. They are compact, slim animals and the Kadazan farmers ride them like horses. Many women working on the roads. They wear a dark square of cloth over their heads and across their faces and they are almost completely masked. This cloth is kept in place by a coolie hat. They look like colourful bandits.

We arrive at a village built on a muddy river. All houses are made of wooden planks with matted roofs standing on stilts of tall, slim tree trunks. Transport is by canoe. Here we see men drying their fishing nets, women preparing food which looks like dried fish. An old lady comes out of her hut, down a broad wooden ladder, steps into a canoe and paddles away across the river.

We drive on and come to a small town. What a feast of sights and sounds! Such a hullabaloo. Children, dogs, tobacco smoke, wood fires, and again the air is filled with the smell of delicious cooking smells. This exotic food is wrapped in enchanting disguises of colour and shapes. Street stalls everywhere.

Women and children are squatting on the ground with their goods displayed all around them, hand-woven baskets in vivid patterns, hats, beadwork and metal jewellery. An old woman is sharing a hand-rolled cigar with another, rekindling an immemorial tradition of loyalty. The farmers bring vegetables and fruits, the fishermen the best of their catch. The town tradesmen offer goods from the factories and ports.

Separated by jungles and days of journeying, bound for most of the week to the soil or the sea, the interior tribes and the town Sabahans must have the market day at least once a week to bring themselves together. Cock fights attract the gamblers but the fights are bloodless. The birds do not wear spurs.

The fish stalls are fascinating. The fish are tied in bundles and come in all shapes and sizes, round, flat, long and thin, brightly coloured, striped, spotted, silvery and some are dried dangling from a length of string like dead leaves. The vendors are passive gazing at us from beneath their coolie hats, wearing brilliant cottons – orange, blue, yellow.

Naked children just stare at us with no commercial interest at all, just curiosity and disbelief. We are both white-skinned, fair-haired and blue-eyed. No cries of 'One dollar please'. The villagers are not keen for us to take photos. A great disappointment but their wishes must be respected.

We leave this throbbing market place and are now on a rough track full of potholes and loose stones. Dropping away to our left is a

We arrive at a village – Sabah.

wide expanse of quarry. There is a mill grinding the huge rocks and convoys of lorries are queuing up to take it away for building. A cluster of galvanised iron huts nestle at the edge of the jungle. Workmens' huts.

We continue along the rough track and come to a 'hanging' bridge spanning the river running parallel to the track. It is extremely flimsy made of wooden planks – some broken, some rotten. We decide we must walk the walk across it just to find out – a nerve-racking experience. There is nothing solid about it. The hand rail is plaited hemp, rather worn and frayed. It's like walking on jelly covered with straw. Below the river swirls and gurgles. I thought of the Bridge of San Luis Rey but the distance to the water churning below was not as distant as in that Peruvian ravine.

Back to the Land-Rover and we continue up the winding mountain track climbing higher all the time. The views across the valley are indescribably beautiful. Every shade of green. The dark green of the wooded hillsides and the incongruous sight of tall, showy plants with yellow flowers tangling with the telephone wires overhead.

Deep ravines drop away to a carpet of trees in velvety valleys and in the distance clusters of wooden huts nestling in clearings on the hill sides. Cattle rest under the houses on stilts which are built on patches of green glades in the jungle. We stop the Land-Rover to savour the sight spread all around us, the stillness disturbed only by bird song or the bleating of a goat.

The butterflies flit from one vivid bloom to another. And then I see it! And then another – there are several of them flitting around my head. Fearless and curious. They are almost as big as a bird. I knew of their existence from my research but had no idea that I would be so lucky as to see them. The Raja Brooke Birdwing (*Ornithopetra brookeana*), black and velvety with brilliant emerald green markings on its wings. It is the largest butterfly I have ever seen. And it is one of the most exciting moments of my life, standing on a jungle track in Borneo with these extraordinary creations fluttering around my head.

Hanging bridge – like walking on jelly covered with straw – Sabah.

We return to the Land-Rover and turn a corner on the rough track and lo and behold! We find a school. Up here, on this mountain side, in the middle of nowhere, miles from a main road, children in smart navy blue tunics and white blouses, carrying navy blue satchels, are just leaving. Others are playing in a green paddock below the school. It is in a clearing with a backdrop of jungle and the entrance gate is a precarious climb up a wooden ladder made of tree trunks.

There is no glass in the windows of the schoolroom. The room is neat and tidy with rows of wooden desks facing a rather small blackboard. Drawings of animals are pinned to the wooden walls.

We decide to walk into the jungle and look for an opening but it's just a thick, matted wall of entangled vegetation, so dense we need machetes to hack our way in. We have no machete so we stay on the narrow muddy footpath. We can hear twigs cracking, shrieks and screams and little noises. Tantalising! There are flowers of every hue on the jungle path and an all-season tree with different-coloured leaves. On one branch the leaves are bronze and dry – autumn. On another there is bright green new growth – spring.

In the undergrowth I find a pitcher plant (*Nepenthes*), so dry it is brown. It has a liquid-containing bowl that traps and digest insects. It looks like a bulbous cup suspended on a delicate stem. I decide to take it home. Back on board I wrap it in cotton wool and tissue paper and yes, I did get it back to Southampton all in one piece. I proudly took it along to the next meeting of my local Natural History Society but the learned Professors from the University just did not believe that I had picked it up in the Borneo jungle and brought it back to England. Pity! I saw these pitcher plants growing in the Seychelles and Papua New Guinea.

In that same thicket of undergrowth I also find something else. It is circular and black metal. I scrape off the soil and can see that it's an old cooking pot. Circumference six inches, four inches deep. A crack in the side of the pot has rendered it quite unserviceable for cooking. It has two fragments of rusty wire on 'buttons' on either side – remnants of the handle for hanging over a fire. It reclines in the bottom of my broom cupboard. Inside I have put a note for my Executrix. I'm sure *she* will believe that I found it in the Borneo jungle. What she will do with it is another matter!

On to another stop. We walk into a wood. This is close by the road and not nearly so dense. It reminds me of the New Forest. Here are the rubber trees. An incision is made into the bark at about waist height then a narrow channel is scored down to the ground where a bowl catches the sap.

Wandering through the trees we come across a small group of huts on stilts with a large clearing where lengths of what looks like creamy coloured plastic about a foot wide and perhaps eight feet long are draped over long wooden poles. Like washing on a clothes line. Rubber drying.

Inside one of the huts an old lady is sitting cross-legged on a table grinding a red substance in a small brass bowl with what looks like a spent cartridge. We decide she's grinding the nuts that so many natives chew. She is very old and has no teeth.

Under the table is an assortment of buckets and pots and pans. On the wall are magazine cuttings (in the heart of the jungle!) and a framed photo of some men. This timeless scene impresses me so much that I wrote a poem and called it 'Dignity'. You will find it at the end of the book.

Moving through this clearing we come to a longhouse. A ridge-roofed building high above the ground on wooden piles with a thatched roof. It is divided lengthwise into an outer hall or corridor and inner family compartments. Entrance is by means of a notched log forming a ladder, rather like the one at the school I have just described. The individual hall serves as a general gathering place. Paddles, fish traps, pots and other articles of daily use are stored here. Apparently, dances for war celebrations, ceremonies and the like are held in the corridor of the long house. A huge earthenware pot, large enough for a child to hide in, stands outside the door of the house.

Creamy coloured strips of plastic – rubber drying Sabah.

Transport is by dugout canoe. Travel through the dense forest is difficult and formerly was hazardous for all but war parties. Wild pig is stalked and hunted with blowpipes. The clouded leopard lives here in the dense tropical forests. And so do honey bears. They attack menstruating women. The orang-utan is found deep in the forests. Timber is the main export. Rice is the staple food. Sabah is rich in minerals – not yet developed.

So we drive back down the mountain track along the winding valleys, through the ranges and hillocks and head for the ship. Reluctantly we have to accept that this is one of the hardest countries in the world to move around on foot.

As we approach the docks I can see Mount Kinabalu, brooding and beckoning in the distance rising above the lush tropical greenery. We didn't get there. Another time perhaps.

I would have liked to explore Tenom, a small town in the heart of rugged countryside and I quote '...where they live the old life style of forest survival, hunt with blow pipes, live in longhouses, chant old songs and dance to the rhythms of the jungle...' There is no road to it but there is a railway – British built, metre gauge, from Tanjong Aru, three miles south of Kota Kinabalu but there just isn't enough time.

Sabah, the land below the wind, a mountainous country of dense tropical forests. The world was beautiful until man polluted it – Sabah is proof. There are no factory whistles – only the lonely bleating of a goat, the swish of oars in water, the peal of children's laughter. And I saw no wild women! It was quite beautiful and quite unique. *Selamat jalan.* Farewell. Till we meet again in mystic, mysterious, lovely Sabah, definitely on my list for another visit.

Bali

The *QE2* anchored off Bali one crystal clear morning in February. The view from the deck is breathtaking, the air is like champagne and the sun bathes us in goodwill. I can see mountains and dense jungle, lush vegetation and a pageant of flowers clinging to hillsides. They look like hanging gardens. Deserted beaches stretch away to port and starboard of the *QE2*. There are temples – there is tropical splendour everywhere.

The scene invigorates me and this sultry, colourful island does not disappoint. Our passengers have gone ashore by launch where they transferred to coaches which have taken them to Denpasar, the capital.

After a couple of hours combing through manifests I am satisfied that I am up to date with invitations for the next round of Reception and Farewell parties so I decide it's time to explore.

I step from the small landing stage and find myself in a narrow street lined with shops and bazaars. The Balinese are out in force plying their trade and selling all kinds of local craftware. Carved coconut shells, ivory carvings, silver filigree work and souvenirs for this invasion by the Western world. I am bemused to see some strange wooden animal carvings for sale on one of the stalls. The carvings depict two goats copulating. How about one of those for Aunt Mary's mantelpiece!

I leave the bazaars behind and walk along the road to the end of the so-called town passing women carrying baskets on their heads, boys on bikes going to school, old men sitting in the shade of trees and youths on noisy motorbikes. Small white houses are set back from the road lined with tall trees and palms. It's getting hotter. Here are the notes I made on that unforgettable day:

'Eventually leave the road and go along a track – with some trepidation. I follow two women swathed in brightly patterned cotton wraps, carrying large, circular straw baskets (empty) on their heads. They disappear into the undergrowth and I find myself at the edge of a wide clearing of thick green vegetation surrounded by more tall trees. Like a forest glade. Suddenly there is such a commotion. The clearing comes to life. I haven't noticed a group of men, women and children bending down cutting the green crop. A dozen or more women and children come towards me, screaming and yelling and waving knives above their heads. I freeze on the spot.

The children get to me first. One teenager is wearing a white bra and a beige cotton skirt. I just stand perfectly still and smile. They mill around me touching my bare arms, my bare legs, they pinch my breasts, they examine my binoculars and camera dangling round my neck. An old woman arrives and stands in front of me. At least she looks old. She is topless, her breasts hanging in brown leather folds below her waist. She has a child in her arms. An old man carrying a knife joins her. I can now see that the knives are more like sickles. He squints at me with his rheumy eyes. He has very bad teeth but he's smiling. Everyone is smiling. There are beautiful butterflies and birds flitting about and I can hear a woodpecker.

So I stand still whilst they walk around me, assessing me rather like the way an animal is inspected at the cattle market.

The men and women lose interest and decide to go back to their work but the children are still prodding and poking. They pull at my dress and keep tugging at it lifting it up and looking underneath. I am wearing just an ordinary coloured cotton print. I don't know whether they want the dress to take away or to see if I am the same colour all over but I knew I must do something to distract them. I ask the way to the sea. They don't understand me.

Close by the footpath is a tree on a small, green hillock so go and sit down to write this but I find it difficult to concentrate with six or more small children jabbering away. They are all girls wearing shabby loose cotton dresses and they are barefoot. It is difficult to guess their age, probably six or seven years old. They are lean and lively.

They have quietened down and are watching me write, their huge brown eyes riveted on me. I offer the pencil and pad to them but they just shake their head and smile. So I draw a sketch of the *QE2* and write the words *Cunard QE2* in capital letters. One of the girls takes the shorthand pad and writes the word 'amlapura'. Then I draw a horse and the same girl writes the words 'mintak wang', and passes the pad back to me.

A man is walking on a footpath close by carrying a wooden table on his head. He stops, puts the table down and comes to watch me writing. He asks for nothing, he simply stands silently looking down at me writing. Now he is squatting not one yard away. I wonder what he wants. Good job he can't read this. He's probably seen the cigarettes in my bag. I don't smoke but give them as gifts ashore. This man has unusually long teeth, bad teeth. His eyes are on my small, zip travel bag. No one has attempted to steal anything. Neither have they asked for anything. All just curious and friendly. I continue to draw birds, butterflies, me at a desk and pass the pad to the children sitting around me, expectant, eager, mystified as they identify first one object then another.

I give the man cigarettes and he goes back to his table, puts it on his head and continues on his way. The children scamper along the narrow path into the jungle. I don't know if the man told the children to go away and leave me.'

After that unexpected encounter I now have time to relax and enjoy my situation sitting on this little green hillock surrounded by lush vegetation, a kaleidoscope of blooms, shrubs, flowering cacti. Swallows and brown birds whoop and circle in the air and I can hear that woodpecker again, deep in the trees. Beautiful butterflies everywhere. Some have orange spots and there are large ones, black and mauve. Some are black and white. There are so many of them fluttering like huge pieces of confetti wafting in the air. I can hear the metallic clang of cow bells, dogs barking, hens cackling, birds singing, crickets chirping. Enormous bumble bees zooming amongst the flowers. I could burst with the pleasure and beauty of it all.

But a lot of work is waiting for me and I must get back to the ship. So I wander along the jungle path, past thatched huts with piles of sawn timber stacked neatly near the door and pigs scuffling around in the clearings. Two small boys are collecting stones in a large woven bowl. I meet a man carrying two magnificent fighting cocks, one under each arm. He puts them down on the track for me to photograph. The birds immediately set about each other so he scoops them up and goes on his way.

Beyond the trees the sea glistens and soon I arrive at a small beach with a rocky overhang. An old fisherman with leaded nets draped over his shoulders poses for me. Some youths stand over a pile of coconuts. They slice one open and drink the milk. Just beyond the rocks the *QE2* is at anchor – she looks marvellous and I am reminded that it's time to return.

Back on board, renewed and stimulated once again, I settle down to solve the problems that beset the passengers with their parties. The number of guests, dates that clash, which champagne to serve and so on but these 'problems' are in the distant reaches of my mind. I am preoccupied with my encounters. I speak no Indonesian but I feel a strong sense of communication with these children, crossing that

I meet a man carrying two splendid fighting cocks – Bali

invisible language divide and the cultures that separate us. We had become friends with nothing more ordinary than a smile. It was delightful to meet these friendly, inquisitive people in their tropical paradise.

Such chance encounters in the jungle could never have been organised by any Tour Operator and that is why I prefer to go wandering alone to find the unexpected, the unplanned, the unscheduled. It's always rewarding.

And as the sun goes down the men, women and children go to their thatched huts, cook a meal on an open fire and the children will go to bed wondering about 'white woman' and the big ship. And the white woman will go to bed in her cabin in a floating metal home wondering why they wanted her cotton dress.

And now these wonderful memories have been scarred by the recent atrocity committed by terrorists on this paradise island. Centuries of tropical splendour have been violated but time will heal, peace will return. The children will smile and wonder again.

Tongatapu

Queen Salote rode in an open carriage at the Coronation of Queen Elizabeth II (1953) and it poured with rain but she sat there smiling and waving and captured the hearts of us all. Now we're tying up at Queen Salote Wharf early in the morning. I've made sure my work is organised so that I can get away to explore this Kingdom in the South Seas. The best way of getting around the island is by horse – I see several men riding bareback but opt for a jeep with a Tongan English-speaking driver, Johnny.

We drive out of the small town, along dirt roads with thatched huts set back under the palm trees. I can see a long-handled besom, hand-made, propped against the door of one hut but there doesn't appear to be much to sweep up. Pigs snuffle around and chickens follow them hopefully.

We haven't been motoring for half an hour when Johnny stops, takes a spanner from under his feet, jumps out and tightens up the nuts on the nearside front wheel. They are working loose on the bumpy roads. I also notice that when he hoots he doesn't touch the steering wheel so I watch the next time. He reaches for a loose wire dangling from the dashboard and pushes it into a hole in the steering column – and hoots! So that's how it's done!

We drive through Taa'Nea, a village scattered with little shacks made of plaited palm leaves. More pigs. Here we see an enormous evergreen tree called ovava. We arrive at a deserted beach. On the left dark rocks covered in foliage rise from the water; on the right are green bushes and shrubs and undergrowth full of birds chattering and singing. There are many thin and mangy dogs sniffing around.

From the beach we drive across the island along deserted roads. The engine overheats so Johnny stops and I go on a mini-safari while it cools down. I follow a narrow, overgrown track into a maze of trees and thick bushes. There are lots of birds, butterflies, dragonflies, flowers and plants. One plant is particularly interesting. Its leaves are feathery, fern-type, growing low on the ground. I push past it. Before my very eyes it shrivels up and looks like a bunch of dead twigs! So I experiment. On touching the leaves with a matchstick they close up and droop instantly. Dead! Wait and after a short while they come back to life again. Fresh and green. Fascinating.

Johnny drives to another beach, also deserted, with a small island in the bay. Heron, snowy egret, sand-piper, moorhen are feeding on the mud flats. Tonga is not noted for its land birds but migratory birds visit some of the less developed islands. And there are more mangy dogs paddling around in the water. A thin black dog splashes into the water and catches a fish then it scrambles up a tree not far from me, flops on to a branch and eats it!

Tonga is on the itinerary the following year and it is humid and overcast when we arrive but the sun does come out after a rain shower. I can't get ashore until midday and only have a couple of hours so hire an open jeep again. This time I want to find the legendary flying foxes (bats with fox-like heads). Joe, the driver, a middle-aged easy-going Tongan, knows where they are.

He drives me past the Royal Tombs situated near the centre of the town. This area has been the burial place of Tongan Royalty since 1893. Joe points out Queen Salote's tomb on a raised dais standing in an open space, surrounded by lawns. As we leave the capital, Nuku'alofa, we pass more burial grounds. Light-coloured gravel mounds, decorated with bright flowers and lengths of chiffon wafting in the breeze.

We drive west along the coast for about eighteen kilometres to the village of Kolovai. Joe pulls up and points to what look like bundles of dried leather in the trees. These are flying foxes hanging upside down, clinging to the branches of the casuarina trees. The trees are very tall with straight trunks and long green branches with small leaves. There must have been 200 or more flying foxes in three trees. They are not asleep. They are restless, squabbling with each other and flapping their black plastic wings as they move along the branches. One flies off, circles around and comes back to roost.

Through my binoculars I can see that these creatures have sandy-coloured furry heads and shoulders. Suspended from the branches they seem to be enveloped in a black umbrella. At night they fly around and feed on mangoes and other fruit. Legend says that the first bats were a gift of a Samoan maiden to an ancient Tongan navigator. The flying foxes are sacred and may be hunted only by members of the Royal Family.

Then from Kolovai we drive to Houma passing the most beautiful flowers and shrubs – frangipani and others I can't identify. On the rocky, terraced coastline at Houma waves crash through the holes in the rocks forcing plumes of spray high into the air through the blow holes. I buy ripe bananas. Very short, fat ones that taste like no banana I have tasted before.

We drive back to Nuku'alofa to browse among the wares offered for sale by the native Tongans. These dignified ladies with their natural charm sit quietly at the roadside, legs stretched out in front of them surrounded by their hand-woven baskets and bowls, weaving and tapa (bark cloth). This is made from the inner bark of trees and beaten with a club over a log of wood to the required thickness. It is then painted and decorated.

There is no yelling, no noise, no waving of arms, no pushing or shoving. The women smile and invite me to look and buy. They are all ages, young and old, dressed in brilliantly coloured cottons. I can't resist the baskets. They are flawlessly crafted and so cheap. I give the lady double the amount she asks – it must have taken her hours and hours to weave such a beautiful basket. And, remember, I'd learnt my lesson in Vera Cruz! I still have the basket and it is in pristine condition.

Everywhere the perfume from the blossoms mingles with the smell of wood-burning fires. It's a glorious, wholesome smell. And all is well with their world. There is free medical and dental treatment. Primary education is free and compulsory between ages six and fourteen years. Everywhere closes on Sundays. There are no newspapers published in Tonga – the Government issues a news sheet daily which is distributed without charge. Tipping is not encouraged. It is an honour to give service to the visitor. This is Tonga.

Before we sail away a Folklore Group comes on board to entertain the passengers. A group of musicians, big bare-chested men in cotton skirts with colourful leis, bring the ship to life with their rhythmic music.

In front of them four girls are swaying and dancing, wearing skirts of wet, green leaves with flowers in their hair, round their wrists and round their ankles. Then they sit down and the men break into a fiery war dance. These men are younger than the musicians. Strong and muscular with shiny brown bodies, all smiling, all enjoying every minute of it. Such happy, happy people. A wonderful finale to a wonderful day amongst these friendly smiling Tongans. Friends of sea and sky and earth.

Papua – New Guinea

Another country to fire the imagination – head hunters! New Guinea has no railways and roads are found near chief towns and plantations so it's got to be four wheels and it's incumbent upon me to get my work boxed off so that I can get away as soon as possible to explore this wild and fascinating country. The people no longer hunt heads but they do cover themselves in mud and they dance in the trees at the Rabaul Warargira festival.

As the *QE2* eases into Port Moresby once again I get cold feet about going alone! A little white head might be quite a novelty! So... I explained my plans to Chuck, a former United States Marine, one of our Terrible Ten. Yes. Without hesitation Chuck agrees to come and we are down the gangway with indecent haste.

I am amazed how modern some of these ports are in such far-flung places. Orderly streets, neat office blocks, luxury hotels. We make a beeline for the Tourist Office. I want to hire a Land-Rover or pickup truck as I had done in Sabah. The attractive young assistant makes several phone calls but is unable to locate a vehicle. I didn't make advance arrangements and I'm beginning to regret it. Precious time is slipping by so we take a taxi to the airport. There's sure to be something on wheels there. After quite a hassle we manage to hire a bright yellow station wagon with driver. Henry (popular name) speaks good English, is wearing a striped shirt with white shorts and no shoes.

We soon get clear of everything that reminds us of the Western world and are driving through deep valleys with purple mountain ranges towering above. Henry pulls up on a track and points to something hanging in a large cage outside a wooden house with a thatched roof. It is a cuscus and looks like a big white and orange cat with thick fur. It's an orange-faced phalanger. Is it a pet, I ask? He doesn't know. Or perhaps he doesn't want to tell us why this animal is caged when its brothers and sisters are hanging free in the forest not far away.

We continue along deserted roads through valleys flanked by ravines bathed by waterfalls. There are rain forests, damp and cool, and distant blue grey mountains wreathed in mist. After about fifty kilometres we turn on to a dirt track. We are entering Varirata National Park. A notice asks us to 'Take nothing but pictures – leave nothing but footprints'.

The Park covers one thousand hectares at an altitude of 860 metres which gives us a very comfortable climate. It stands on land of the Koiari people and was created in 1963 after consultation with the local Koiari leaders. This is the land of their grandfathers and is full of the history, legend and culture of these people. They are proud that their land has been chosen as the site for the first National Park of New Guinea, protected by the Government. With harmony and consultation instead of bulldozing officials, public enquiries, confrontations and protests. It can be done. I salute the Koiari.

We decide to park and walk. Henry comes with us and I notice that he remains barefoot as we wander the tracks and pathways with the rain forest on one side and the savannah woodland stretching away on the other. There are a lot of birds which are difficult to see but we can hear their unusual calls. Wailings and screeches and melodious refrains. Bandicoots and wild pigs live here. And brown pythons. There are two pigs' nests in the open savannah where the pigs come to raise their young. Visitors are asked not to damage them because they are used again and again.

We see all kinds of flowers and coloured thistles and vines and canes in the undergrowth. One tall plant looks like a flowering corn on the cob. More than two-thirds of the world's orchids are found in Papua New Guinea

We arrive at a spectacular waterfall and get drenched with spray at the viewing balcony. Henry's feet are now very muddy! We gaze into deep ravines, wild and wooded, with a river snaking its way through the valley into a lake. There are snowy egrets near the river, and fish eagles hanging their wings out to dry. Fruit bats dangle from the trees. We come to a huge grey rock on a grassy escarpment. It is cracked from top to bottom as if it had been thrown down from the heavens and broken open on impact. A small tree is growing in the cleft.

There are miles and miles of track and rain forest and savannah to be explored but we have to head back to Port Moresby for sailing.

Just off Ela Beach on the corner of Musgrave Street are two War Memorials. One is in the form of a rectangular granite archway inscribed with the names of 129 residents who were enlisted in 1914 – 1918. Towards the hillside is another plaque commemorating the people of Papua New Guina who served in the 1939 – 1945 War.

It had been quite a hassle to find the vehicle but very rewarding to walk in this extraordinarily unspoilt world of natural beauty.

The following year Papua New Guinea was included on the itinerary again and, having learned a trick or two, I worked out what I wanted to do on arrival. I was going to hire a vehicle and go to the Chimbu and Eastern Highlands but the best laid schemes of mice and men... the Captain announced trouble with the boilers and our call at Port Moresby was cancelled. We continued on reduced speed to Manila.

Manila

This disruption to the itinerary causes grumbles from some of the passengers but there are no serious complaints. They are enthralled with the sights and sounds of these fascinating islands and there are more to come. I am too busy to plan anything adventurous in Manila. We have a lot of embarks so I know I can't go ashore for long but once I have my work under control I decide to have a look at this bustling, thriving city. And I had the most extraordinary luck as I left the ship.

The quayside is large and wide and clean and tidy. Exceptionally clean and tidy. And it is crowded with excited families, men, women, children, brightly dressed. Men in pristine white uniforms with lots of gold braid are mingling with the crowd. Police are strutting up and down. A band is playing – not for us – we docked hours ago and the passengers are already ashore sightseeing. The crowd is getting excited.

Clearly something big is about to happen so I hang about at the bottom of the gangway and then... with a great fanfare of trumpets a long, sleek, white yacht comes gliding alongside. It is bedecked with flags fluttering from bow to stern. The after deck is a garden of flowers and garlands of every colour, the awnings and supporting poles entwined with blossoms. An incredible sight. Who on earth does this belong to?

Then I saw her... an elegant, slim woman with jet black hair, wearing a pale blue full length dress of what looks like brocade. She is waving and smiling to the crowds. It's Imelda Marcos, wife of the President. She steps on to the gangway, which is level with the quayside, but I cannot see which shoes she is wearing! Then she slides elegantly into the waiting limousine and is gone with police escort and motor cycle outriders, klaxons blazing!

Once again, the unexpected! I make my way into town along a wide, open waterfront with modern, high-rise hotels, surrounded by green lawns, shrubs and flowers. As I get into the city centre it is wall to wall traffic. Such chaos as you could never imagine with much hooting and tooting and people hanging out of little gaudily-painted buses, decorated with chrome knobs with the locals boarding from an opening at the rear.

There are motor cycles, taxis, trucks. What a razzmatazz. The noise is deafening. I really don't need this so I escape to a Spanish tea room and watch it all from a window table before making my way back to the *QE2*. When I get to the quayside the Presidential yacht has gone.

Tahiti

Yet another early docking brings us to a different island paradise in the South Pacific. The harbour is full of ships of the French Navy. I knew they were here but am surprised they are here in such force. Sleek, grey vessels armed to the gunnels with unidentifiable masterpieces of modern warfare. On a beautiful, peace-loving island like this! Somehow it doesn't mix.

I have a lot of work to do. After sailing all passengers travelling alone are invited to cocktails. So I have to comb through the manifests to find their names, confirm room numbers, address the envelopes, sort them by deck and make sure they are delivered. A lot of checking and scribbling. But I just have to set foot on terra firma if only for a few hours.

Off I go in bright sunshine, a cobalt blue sky, an island full of colour, music and flowers. Not far from the dock sensuous South Sea islanders dance and sway in their grass skirts and garlands to revitalize the passengers. And the handsome, chunky men with pixie ears beguile us all.

The local children, happy and well fed, dart hither and thither amongst this unusual cargo that has come ashore, excited at this invasion.

I wander around the sleepy streets. There is very little traffic – it is Sunday. I find a footpath and follow it for some distance, climbing all the time. I can hear birds in the trees but the only bird I can see is a pigeon. Back to the invitations.

We sailed at six o'clock in the evening and I went on deck to watch this island melt away. Alan, one of the Radio Officers was taking the air, too, and he told me about a strange thing that had happened as we approached Tahiti.

He explained that the *QE2* has the call sign of the *Queen Mary*, long out of service but this morning, 5th February 1978, *QE2* received a radio message in Morse concerning the *Queen Mary's* position in the North Atlantic. The *Queen Mary* sailed from Southampton for the last time on 31st October 1967, eleven years ago! Destination Long Beach. The signal had been into the atmosphere and bounced back off 'something' to be picked up by *QE2* – discuss!

I was told that this news item featured on BBC Radio Solent, our local radio station in Southampton.

It was a balmy evening and a silky breeze ruffled the ocean. The sky was full of stars and it came home to me once again that there are more mysteries out there than any human can begin to comprehend. The *Queen Mary* long gone from sailing the oceans, sends *QE2* a message! What next!

Hawaii

Sailing across the Pacific Ocean under a huge cloudless sky we arrive at a chain of islands – the Sandwich Islands – Hawaii. They were discovered by Polynesians but Captain James Cook was the first European to visit in 1778.

More than two hundred years later *QE2* follows in his wake and headed for Oahu where we dock at Honolulu. Oahu is diamond shaped with two immense volcanoes but erosion has formed two rugged parallel mountain ranges. We nudge alongside the quay sheltered by lush, green palm trees, thickly wooded mountains forming a backdrop to the city skyscrapers, tall, white glistening towers. Hotels, office blocks, luxurious apartment blocks.

Here in Hawaii the prosperity and affluence of the West has been blended and stirred in a melting pot to give the best of both worlds – the smiling, friendly people have not compromised the relaxed, unhurried tempo of their fantastic island.

This year the QE2 has made a clockwise circumnavigation of the world and by the time Hawaii is on the horizon we are nearly home and I'm exhausted.

It's an overnight port and I decide to pack a bag and get away from it all. Angela, the Interpreter, pops into my cabin and catches me in the act. She is off-duty, can she come with me? So off she went to pack a bag. Don't tell anyone.

Think of Hawaii and I think of the white powdery Waikiki beach, Diamond Head, the turquoise blue water, luxury hotels, exciting restaurants and night clubs, the lilting music, grass skirts, colourful leis – but that's the affluent tourist scene.

I want to get away from all that so we head for the Tourist Office and get a map. A bus service makes a complete tour of the island. We pick out a place called Laie on the north-east coast and head for it.

The bus takes us across the island passing fields and fields of pineapples, sugar cane, dairy farms and ranches. We drive through tropical forests and lush valleys – there are no snakes. These scenes don't appear in the glossy brochures.

Hawaii is an agricultural island. Tourism is the third largest source of income after pineapples and sugar cane, not forgetting coffee and rice. Since the highest quality of pineapple is not developed except when the pineapple fruit is allowed to become fully ripe on the plant, fresh fruit quality is impaired by long shipment! You have been warned. I love fresh pineapple so this gem of wisdom intrigued me.

On arrival at Laie, a small coastal town, we have difficulty in finding a room. We try two hotels. They are fully booked but a helpful receptionist makes a phone call and we are lucky at Laniloa Lodge Hotel. It has a private beach and the surf riders are having a wonderful time. Beyond them, far away towards the horizon we can see whales blowing. Next morning I wake to the noise of the sea pounding on the beach and birds singing in the trees.

After breakfast we have to be on the move to get back for duty. The bus continues round the northern tip and on to Waimea Falls often referred to as the 'Little Grand Canyon of the Pacific'. Then across the island back to Honolulu.

There are places we didn't visit – Pearl Harbour to the west of Honolulu. It is still an important Naval Base –and I didn't know it was a land-locked harbour.

So after our taste of paradise it's back to five hundred cocktail invitations… and as we sail away from the beaches and palm trees the ladies are on deck, lifting their leis over their recently coiffured hair and throwing them into the sea. The Polynesians believe that if they float towards the shore it means the visitor will return!

South America

Panama

The clattering and banging and hooting of whistles waken me at 7a.m. We are slipping under the Bridge of The Americas at the port of Balboa heading for Miraflores Locks.

Charles I of Spain ordered the first survey of a proposed canal route through the Isthmus of Panama. The work was started three centuries later by the French in 1880 but disease and financial problems defeated them. The Canal is fifty miles long and was first opened on 15 August 1914. It was owned, operated and controlled by the United States under treaty until 31 December 1999, when ownership was transferred to the Panamanians.

I have transited the Panama Canal nineteen times and it never fails to impress me. There is much development on reclaimed land on either bank and as I write the Panamanians have just voted to widen the Canal to enable the massive new container ships to transit (2006). Watch this space. It will be a costly venture.

The most interesting part of this monumental achievement is the Gaillard Cut through the Continental Divide. During construction it was called Culebra Cut but renamed for Colonel David DuBose Gaillard, the engineer in charge of this nine mile section of the Canal work. It was hewn through rock and shale for most of that distance.

The human cost was enormous. Disease claimed the lives of thousands of workmen. On the rock face called Contractor's Hill there is a large plaque to honour the memory of the men who perished. William Crawford Gorgas, a US Army Surgeon, contributed greatly by introducing mosquito controls to prevent yellow fever and malaria.

Cruise liners transit during the day for the benefit of passengers – there are some good photo opportunities – but cargo ships generally go through at night. It is quite, quite spectacular with high mast lighting in all lock areas and the jungle is iridescent with lights all along the banks on either side. But beware – mosquitoes come out at night! They like dank, swampy water.

As we progress through the Gatún Lake to Gatún Locks we can see small settlements on either side of the Canal and beyond them more dense jungle. A railway line connects Cristóbal and Balboa and runs parallel with the Canal. Several times during the day a bright blue diesel train speeds along with a toot, toot here and a toot, toot there.

Movement is s l o w and once in the lock we are stationary. I was in my cabin at one stage and watched the rough grey wall of the lock slipping past my porthole. I estimate the wall was no more than twelve inches from the skin of the *QE2!*

The team of personnel getting this huge liner through the locks is very smart and efficient. They wear brown overalls and bright yellow hard hats. All appear to be the same height and shape and they remind me of clever beetles. They come on board as we enter the first lock and work in total harmony with another team who operate the locomotives on shore.

Lines are thrown from the ship and anchored to these sturdy locomotives, called mules, which pull us slowly into the lock. Our passage through the Canal attracts crowds of people at the landing stages and we can almost shake hands with them. The average transit time through the Canal is nine hours and at 4p.m. I recognise Cristóbal.

Shore leave is granted and passengers are soon down the gangway. A group of us – Bryan, the Social Director and one or two other members of the staff – decide to go ashore to stretch our legs. At the bottom of the gangway we pause. An ambulance with lights flashing and klaxons blazing screeches to a halt at our feet.

One of our passengers has been attacked. He and his wife were just a short distance from the docks, walking towards the shops when he felt a tug at the back of his trousers. Instinctively he put his hand to his back pocket. The thief was in the process of cutting out the

QE2 enters Panama Canal

pocket with a sharp knife. The passenger's hand got in the way and was badly slashed with blood dripping all over the place. The thief made off with the wallet.

We get the passenger and his terrified wife back on board to the hospital for treatment. And that was the end of our visit ashore.

Venezuela

La Guaira is well known to the ship's company as it was a regular port of call for the *Mauretania* Caribbean cruises and the port of my finest hour on the Bridge! It has not changed much. Those brooding mountains still tower over the port but there seem to be more modern buildings and more back street squalor. The old road that used to snake through the hills has been made-over and the new highway speeds us to Caracas in forty minutes – past the abject shanty settlements clinging to the hillsides – they are still there.

With regular calls at La Guaira we get to know the essentials. Our favourite restaurant, Timotes, is still there – serving the most delicious lobster and, wait for it, Casa Scholl, where feet can be revived for the acres of walking up and down metal decks. We are such regular visitors that the Receptionist keeps Record Cards for us as if we lived just around the corner. Fee $6.00.

It's wonderful to sit there with feet in a jacuzzi, purring with relief, while the handsome young man massages and soothes and reconstitutes my feet for the next eighty days. Divine. No return to the ship can surpass that at La Guaira. Walking on feathers and full of good food and wine at Timotes – who needs feet?

Cartagena – Columbia

You can see the mellow ochre walls and fortresses of the old town as the ship approaches Boca Chica to dock at Cartagena. They were built in the sixteenth century to withstand attacks from the corsairs who sailed these very waters. Great fleets called here annually to take on gold for Spain. Cartagena was also a major market for African slaves. Now the commerce is petroleum. The taxi driver told me that water is more expensive than petrol!

Cartagena is a mix of old and new, rich and poor. There is a quiet dignity about the old town. It seems timeless with its narrow, picturesque streets with flowering plants cascading over the carved balconies.

Old men sitting in the shade in Plaza Bolívar, idle youths hanging around in groups, children and dogs playing in the fountains. It is minding its own business and leaving the modern world to its self-induced frenzy.

The Gold Museum is well worth a visit but be prepared to surrender everything except the clothes you stand up in. Security is tight. Inside, those artefacts are pure gold, made centuries before a pair of spectacles adorned a nose and electricity lit a workshop.

The Museum of Modern Art with its avant-garde exhibitions is, perversely, in one of the oldest buildings in the Plaza de la Aduana. It has weathered timber double-doors shackled with cast iron bolts and stone walls more than four feet thick.

Time for me to get back to the ship. There is a string of taxis lined up next to the open air flower market.

I ask the driver, 'How much to Puerto Maritimo?'

'Three dollar.' He is good-looking (most of them are) sturdily built, swarthy, late thirties. He stares at me and I notice his eyes are not focussed. They are all over the place, not on this planet. There is a dangerous gloss about this man. Is it drink or drugs? I have to extricate myself from this contract.

'*Bueno*, I still have some shopping to do. I'll be back later.'

I wander across to the flower market and buy a huge bouquet of red carnations then I find another taxi, check the driver and he skilfully noses his way through the narrow, old streets.

We are now driving along the coast road to the Maritime port. Hundreds of flimsy shacks have been built on the mud flats at the edge of the turquoise sea on my right.

'Do people live there?' I ask.

'*Si*, but when there's a heavy tide the shacks are washed away.'

Sailing down to Rio

Of all the continents I want to visit, South America holds a special fascination for me, particularly the west coast and the ancient sites of the Inca and pre-Columbian civilisations, but Cunard didn't go there during my years before the mast. I had to wait quite a while before I set foot in Peru.

We are sailing around the world in an anti-clockwise direction on this World Cruise. After leaving New York, Port Everglades, Curacao and La Guaira we skirt the coast of Brazil and head for Salvador Bahia.

It is the oldest city and first capital of Brazil. The capital was transferred to Rio de Janeiro in 1763. I only have a few hours ashore as there is a big reception to prepare for Rio. You will remember that I mentioned it earlier – the Fashion Show and all that jazz and diamond jewellery – but I'm determined to go down that gangway. Gill, one of the Nursing Sisters is off duty so we go together.

The city is divided into two sections – the lower part where the port and commercial districts are located at the foot of the cliff. The principal shopping districts, municipal Government offices and residential areas are on the upper level. There are a few winding roads, a funicular and several elevators to take us there but we decide to stay in the lower town. Churches and beggars abound.

Traffic is a nightmare, roaring along at terrifying speeds and very noisy. We find a covered market selling everything – hammocks are popular, baskets, tortoiseshell, tin trinkets, jewellery. We didn't buy.

Salvador was the major centre of the African slave trade in the colonial period and we saw where they were landed and auctioned to planters. It sends shivers down my spine.

African and European cultures seem to blend smoothly here, from Creole with those uncanny transparent eyes, to Indian. There is a lot of exploring to be done but we have no time and sail south for Rio this evening.

Rio de Janeiro

It is hot and humid and raining when we dock. Sugar Loaf Mountain, that huge solid cone, stands in rain-soaked glory, and Corcovado, the sharp rocky peak, is lost in the mist but it's there with that imposing statue of Christ, 98 feet high and weighing over a thousand tons – a marvel of man-power and engineering.

I manage to go down the gangway for a few hours during the afternoon and stroll along the Avenida Rio Branco, more than a mile long, lined with brazilwood trees. It cuts across the old city. I almost trip over a young man squatting on the pavement. It is made entirely of mosaic tiles but many are broken and uneven and he is tediously mending the holes with small cubes of coloured stone and glass. He has a lot to do.

I arrive at Flamengo Park, an enormous area reclaimed from the sea, and am surprised to find a Monument to the Dead of World War II. Three stone figures of men, representing the Army, Navy and Air Force. They are tall and stylised, standing on a raised square plinth about four feet from the ground. I had no idea that Brazilians fought in World War II. A little research was necessary!

Under the leadership of President Vargas they declared war against Germany and Italy on 22 August 1942. The Brazilian troops distinguished themselves in several battles, especially that of Monte Castello, Italy. I have seen War Memorials in so many of the countries I've visited. It truly was a World War.

But I have to go back to work. The traffic is delirious, tearing along in a frenzy of braking and accelerating, raucous hooting, and clouds of black exhaust fumes. Buildings are being knocked down in a haze of dust. And poor people everywhere. Awful poverty. Worn out women with babies in their arms, begging.

I have to attend an important VIP Reception in the evening with all the bigwigs from Rio – Admirals and Ambassadors – with their gold braid and cockaded hats – and the ladies in their elegant gowns and jewellery. Quite an occasion and, of course, the conversations are in faultless English.

I am disappointed with what I saw of Rio which wasn't very much. I didn't see one handsome man or a single well-dressed woman. I was expecting a chic, cosmopolitan city like Madrid but my time ashore was limited so it is perhaps unfair to make a judgement on such a fleeting visit.

After sailing, my bedroom steward, who has been with Cunard for years, tells me that he and his mate had been ashore.

'How did it go, Bert?' I asked

'Me and Stan went to Copacabana beach.' Bert sniffed. 'Took some beers. Eyed the dollies. By Christ, what dollies! Then we fell asleep.'

'Dangerous in that sun,' I said.

'Nah, Miss. We was O.K. But I never want to see Copacabana beach again.'

'Why is that?' I was going to be late for duty but wanted to know about this fabulous beach.

'Well, when we packs up to return to the ship the beach was deserted. Everybody gone. Not a soul. So we see a narrow footpath to the far right of the beach and heads for it.' Bert wipes his brow. 'But... but when we got closer... when we got closer we could see that it wasn't a footpath. We took one look and scarpered. It were rats on the march.'

During the night, a few hours after leaving Rio, I wake up. The ship's engines have stopped. There is no reassuring throb, no steady vibration. I wonder why but fall asleep again. When I get to the office

I learn that we had sucked in so much garbage and rubbish floating in Rio harbour that it took three hours to unblock the pipes and bilges.

And another problem surfaces during the day. We discover that counterfeit twenty dollar bills are being passed on board!

Uruguay

There is quite a buzz among the senior members of the ship's company as we steam into the River Plate. Many of them have vivid and personal memories of the action here in South America! In World War II? More research needed. This is what I learned.

In December 1939, the *Admiral Graf Spee,* a heavily-armed German battleship, was in action in the South Atlantic with three British light cruisers *(Ajax, Achilles* and *Exeter).* The *Admiral Graf Spee* was so damaged she had to seek shelter in the neutral waters of the River Plate. When the Government of Uruguay ordered her to leave Captain Hans Langsdorff destroyed his own ship and allowed the crew to be interned. He then committed suicide. The film *Battle of the River Plate* has a different version. Captain Langsdorff survived.

Once again the *QE2* sails over another ship's grave. So many war memorials around the world, so many graveyards, so many memories... where have all the flowers gone? As if we didn't know!

We nose our way alongside the quay in Montevideo, a city softened by age with long, grassy slopes rising gently to the far-off hills.

This is another 'inaugural' port and a big reception is planned. There is great excitement with much coming and going and a lot of panics behind the scenes. More invitations. More cold canapés. More champagne. The President of Uruguay is to be received on board.

All instructions are meticulously followed and at last the limousines arrive and spill the entourage on to the quayside. Uniforms bristle with gold braid and medals. Plumes on hats waft in a light breeze. Ladies elegantly swathed and perfumed trip up the gangway.

In my mind's eye I had created an image of what the President would look like. I decided he would be sturdily built, handsome with greying hair at the temples, dark eyes, moustache, possibly wearing spectacles, middle-aged. How wrong I was! A frail, spindly man with a shock of white hair fixes me with his clear blue eyes. He looks just like my maternal grandfather, George Kirk!

I meet the wife of the Foreign Minister, the Secretary of State and other members of the Diplomatic Corps. It's all very easy and very relaxed with no language problem. I'm always impressed with their impeccable command of English. It's been a long old day, up at crack of dawn to get this event organised and now mixing and mingling with these interesting Uruguayans but I wouldn't have missed a minute of it. I didn't set foot on the gangway and saw nothing of Montevideo except the dockside!

Down Under

New Zealand

Our arrival in the South Pacific has been eagerly awaited and the passengers are enthralled with all the new sights and sounds. Now we are well and truly down under but first we are going to steam around the Bay of Islands on New Zealand's North Island. There is no shore leave but many photo opportunities to capture these little green islands dotted in the deep blue bay.

Zane Grey, the prolific American writer of classic Western novels, made Otehei Bay his base for deep-sea fishing. His lodge is now used as a lunch rendezvous for tourists. I was lucky enough to visit his log cabin in the pine forests of Payson, Arizona where he 'loved the wild canyons and the vast open reach of the desert'. A wonderful place to write creatively but Otehei Bay is a far cry from those wild canyons.

We dock at Auckland at eight o'clock in the morning. It's a lovely open city, easy to navigate. Houses with Victorian bay windows next to slim skyscrapers. There are elegant department stores. No crowds, no one tearing about, no one working on their next stomach ulcer. Everyone with time to walk leisurely, eat leisurely, drink leisurely. And so neat and tidy. I didn't see any litter in the streets. In the UK we wade ankle-deep through discarded soft drink cans and polystyrene burger boxes. Few people sit around a table and eat a civilised meal – they feed on the wing and drop their litter in the street.

I wander along Queen Street until I find the Art Gallery where I spend the whole afternoon looking at work by Brueghel, Reynolds, Cornelius Johnson, Italian and French Masters. Skip this bit if you're not interested in art. One of my shipmates, Sally McDougall played golf on all the golf courses around the world, dodging snakes in bunkers in India. I prefer Art Galleries – you have been warned!

There are paintings depicting Maori life by Gottfried Lindauer

(1839–1926). One in particular fascinates me. It is a big painting (92ins x 74ins) titled 'Tattooing: The Tohunga-Ta-Moko at work'. The tattooist is working on a man lying on his side on a thin raffia mat, identical to the one I slept on in the Buddhist Monastery. You can read about this in the China chapter if you are still with me! The man is sturdily built, bare-chested, wearing a cream-coloured skirt, yes, I do mean skirt. His head rests on the crossed legs of the tattooist who is piercing his face with a long instrument in each hand. Both of these men have black hair but the tattooist, whose face is intricately tattooed, has a grey beard.

Close by, another man is sitting cross-legged on a similar mat. He is quite elderly, wearing a loose robe of cream with a broad black collar, and is holding a wooden spear in his right hand. He has receding grey hair and a thick moustache. They are in a wooden hut with a neatly rolled bundle of dried grass dangling from the ceiling in one corner.

In the foreground is a low seat in deep red, ornately carved with a figurehead at one end. The paint colours are subdued and harmonious – beige, brown, black, dark red – an illustration of Maori culture captured for us on this huge canvas. The postcard was 'An Auckland City Art Gallery Postcard'.

I also saw one of the most striking pictures I have ever seen. It engages the emotions of the viewer spontaneously. A funeral party, ladies and children, on a quayside. On closer inspection it is apparent that the two ladies, wearing white, are carrying a tiny coffin draped in white and yellow. Little girls in white and yellow dresses and hats lead the procession; a group of scruffy urchins with bags of vegetables and bundles of wood watch from a short distance. The emotion between all children is palpable. I asked about the artist – no one knew – but the quayside is somewhere in Cornwall.

A steady overnight passage brings us to Wellington. I am busy with the special parties and hundreds of cards – it's St Valentine's Day! I get anonymous red roses and a box of chocolates! At last I clear my desk and go ashore to meet Joan, a New Zealand friend who used to work for English Electric in New York, the parent company of Marconi's.

We would meet each time the ship docked and I always brought a bottle of lemon barley water for her – unobtainable in America. Any item taken ashore has to be declared on a Customs Declaration Form and stamped by the authorities. I had trouble with this innocuous fruit drink in a bottle. The Customs Officer always interrogated me – 'Is it alcoholic?' – and each voyage I had to convince him that it was not.

We haven't met for seventeen years but she is instantly recognisable and off we go on a tour of Wellington. The War Memorial, the unusual addition to Parliament Buildings, The Beehive, aptly described and very contemporary. Sir Basil Spence was the Consultant. Then to the Lady Norwood Rose Gardens and Begonia House. Wellington is hilly and wooded, open and fresh, a lovely Victorian city. Back to the *QE2*. I have no lemon barley water for her today but after a few glasses of champagne seventeen years slip into oblivion.

The next day there is thick mist as we enter the fjords of Milford Sound on the south-west coast of South Island. But we get lucky – by midday it has lifted and the scenery is breathtaking. Ships enter through a narrow passage banked by dark grey walls rising sheer from the water. Helicopters and light aircraft fly perilously close to the cliff face. The clarity of the sky and the brilliant sunshine make it a photographer's paradise. Every jagged rock and runnel in needle-point relief. We had a very satisfied group of passengers after the day's cruising in Milford Sound. No problems.

Tasmania

We seem to step even further away from the Victorians when we dock at Hobart, founded in 1803 by Lieutenant Collins. Tranquil, with wide open squares, trees, fountains, colourful street markets. Such a quiet, orderly place with amiable, smiling people. The clock has stopped and no one is in a hurry to fast forward it.

I go ashore at midday and walk along the waterfront chatting with the fishermen selling their morning catch from boats moored bow to stern.

I spot a dozen or so fearsome looking fish like small sharks on the deck of a boat. Silvery, large, ugly.

'What are these fish called?' I asked the handsome man with the weather-beaten face.

'Couta.' he grinned up at me. 'Fresh couta.'

'They look so menacing. How do you catch them?'

'With a large hook. No bait. They attack the hook. They're very aggressive.'

On the roof of the wheelhouse of each boat along the waterfront are large white notices announcing the day's catch 'Fresh tasty Trevally Fillets. Deep Sea Flake. Whole Trevally Flake, Today's Fresh Couta $2.00 each.' Clearly these fishermen are adept at provoking a fight with the couta.

I find the Tasmanian Museum of Art. Here I am again. Skip it if you want to. A drab, faceless piece of modern architecture strangely out of kilter with its environment but it does not disappoint inside. I was particularly impressed with one picture – Hobart Town 1868 – by George F. Slade. The landmarks and buildings have changed little since that scene was painted more than a hundred years ago. I have seen a painting of Toledo in the Prado, Madrid and it, too, is completely unchanged. More than we can say for London! Chatting with one of the attendants in the Gallery I discover that he hails from Lincolnshire – Mr Squires from Holbeach, knew my sister-in-law, Pauline Staff and family. The world gets smaller and smaller...

I return to the waterfront and sit on a bollard near the ship to watch the fishermen again, the children playing on the quayside, the women going about their shopping. I just want to drink in this placid, timeless scene. A young man comes over to talk to me. He is from Australia and he and his wife moved to Tasmania three years ago – they love it. Who wouldn't?

In the distance rugged Scottish-type highlands beckon. Blue-grey with a hint of mist under a sky full of lazy clouds. I long to go there, I need more time, more time.

Sydney

An early arrival (one hour before schedule) finds me in bed as the Sydney Bridge slides past my porthole. Panic! But I am on deck in time for docking. A Pipe Band and huge crowds of people are on every square foot of space to welcome us.

And there it is. That majestic collection of shells that seems to have emerged from the depths of the harbour, with layers of symmetrically designed curves in harmonious juxtaposition with the sweep of the Sydney Harbour Bridge. Everything has been said and written about the Opera House but to see it is just breathtaking. Later in the day I was in a park and there, beyond the trees, were the tips of these shells, rising above the trees.

It is the start of an exciting day – phone calls from friends who own an international employment agency, Centacom, with an office in London. They meet me with a car and give me a wonderful tour of Sydney and environs. Camp Cove is where Governor Phillip first landed on 21 January 1768. Now women bathe topless here. On to The Gap at Watson's Bay – the entrance to Sydney Harbour – and the favourite suicide spot. Low tide exposes the rocks that rise sheer out of the water. They look like huge tablets laid out below, so well proportioned I thought they must be man-made. I shudder at the thought of leaping down to them.

We continue along a cliff road above a lighthouse to Dover Heights and then we stop to gaze on a wide crescent of pale sand below edged with white frills and blue, blue sea. Yes, this is it. That famous arc of sand is Bondi Beach. Not crowded – plenty of room for everyone.

This is another of our rare overnight ports. It gives us that longed-for breather in our eighty-day week and the next day my Spanish friend, Consuelo, and her husband Roy, collect me at the ship. Consuelo and I had both worked for Marconi Española in Madrid. She went to Australia and met and married Roy. I went back to England and became a sailor and here we are after all those years. In Australia of all places!

We drive through the Sydney suburbs with very English names – Surrey Hills, Waterloo, Kensington to Botany Bay. Roy used to catch fish here as a boy. A lot of shrubs and bushes grow around the Bay and Roy says there were many snakes here and an old man was adept at catching them. He put them in a bag and showed them to the tourists who willingly rewarded him for his courage. Now the area is being developed, much to Roy's chagrin. Oil refineries, artificial breakwaters with an airport close by and the old man with his bag of snakes has gone.

We drive north through forests to Gosford. For as far as the eye can see there are eucalyptus trees growing amongst the rocks and I am not surprised that bush fires are such a hazard. Full of oil they burn fiercely. Outside the metropolis of Sydney fire fighting services are voluntary.

A modern highway has been cut through the rocks and all along the route there are pull-in areas where fruit and vegetables are sold. Oranges, peaches, apples, pears, plums, grapes – an abundance of produce – all fresh. We drive to a nearby lake and eat fresh prawns watched by a flock of drooling pelicans.

Then it's back to Sydney for a super Spanish meal – just like old times in Madrid – *anda que* – and *QE2* sailed at seven o'clock in the evening.

Hundreds and hundreds of boats escort us. Huge crowds of

Pelicans drool over our fresh prawns on Lake Tuggerah, north of Sydney, Australia

people everywhere. They are hanging from lamp-posts, swinging from trees. Lights flashing, sirens hooting, streamers, music. We get wonderful receptions and farewells all around the world but I don't think I've ever seen anything to equal our departure from Sydney harbour.

Later I go on deck to absorb the events of my first visit down under. The thrill of meeting long lost friends again in Wellington and Sydney. Above is a full moon – very large, very low, very deep gold.

When I get to the office the next morning we discover that we are one passenger short. A retired professor, aged 83. His wife, his passport and all belongings are on board. Cables are sent to the Agent who informs the Police and the Missing Persons procedure is set in motion.

A few hours later we get news that a man has been found in a hospital in Sydney, claiming that he's 63 years old and has nothing to do with the *QE2*. However, his identity is established. We've found our missing Professor. It seems he walked down the gangway with the crowds of visitors leaving the ship before we sailed. He had to fly with a medical escort to our next port, Manila, to rejoin the *QE2* and his wife had to pay all costs and transportation.

The next morning *QE2* is sailing off the Great Barrier Reef. The sky is overcast but there are many passengers on deck to see the myriad of atolls and islands like rugged green cones serrating the horizon.

I have to go to the Bridge on official business – lucky me. The Pilot points out the different islands and I am able to identify them with the charts. So I have the greatest view in the world of this fantastic stretch of water that Captain Cook had navigated. He had to throw six four-pounder guns overboard here to lighten the *Endeavour* when she struck the reef in 1770. The Bridge of the *QE2* bristles with high-tech gear to get us safely through these waters. Captain Cook could never have dreamed of such a Bridge – or could he?

Singapore

Diary note (20 February 1979): 'We docked at midday on a clear and sunny morning. I counted 70 ships at anchor.' It's all very modern and busy and noisy. Once again the apartment buildings, office blocks and hotels rise from the bay like white and silver towers for as far as the eye can see. The harbour, the skyline, the skyscrapers give a depressing 'sameness' as we approach.

Singapore means Raffles Hotel to me and I've waited a long time to fulfil this particular ambition to visit but first there is work to be done.

My friend, Carlos, the South African doctor who became a crew member in Sabah wants to come ashore with me here so we take a bus from the Docks to Orchard Street and walk along pavements with deep gulley drains.

After our abortive attempt to get to Mount Kinabalu in Sabah this visit is mundane. We find a market and buy plums then go to the Mandarin Hotel to wash them in the cloakroom. Most unusual architecture, like an ice cream wafer with a revolving dome which is a restaurant on top. We sit in their gardens and eat the plums!

Then we take a taxi to Chinatown. It is teeming with life. Men and women, young and old, children. Everybody doing something, everybody working. I watch two old women, dressed from head to foot in black. One is helping the other to get a splinter out of her finger without success so she takes an enormous knife to it! I look away and keep walking.

An old man is breaking a large block of ice. He uses an axe to mark it then a metal wedge and a wooden mallet. The ends of two fingers on his left hand are missing.

All along the streets are open-fronted shops selling all manner of unidentifiable food. Chemists with contraceptives on display, magazine stalls with books back to front. Rickshaws. Bicycles with sidecar. Street cafes serving Chinese food. People eating quickly with chopsticks. Women examining live chickens in a crate. The smell of incense mingles with meat cooking, fish cooking, stale urine, cigarette smoke.

Back on board there is a display of Folklorique Malaysian dancing in the Queen's Room. Three girls in bright yellow and red are performing the Chinese Fan Dance. Then a dance by six girls with parasols. It is all so aesthetically pleasing. Six more girls in peacock blue dresses have small cymbals, like metal castanets, on their fingers and dance a most sensuous dance. The Dragon Dance is exciting. The scarlet and gold costume, the large, thrusting head of the dragon, the leaps, the shaking body lunging into the crowd, the punctuated music – it is all vibrant and rhythmic and menacing!

Now comes a man wearing a long brown shirt and a white turban carrying a wicker basket with a lid. There are three snakes in the basket. One is a Malaysian black mamba, the other two are greeny-grey. He drapes them all around his neck and arms. They seem very stiff, not loose and slimy. He invites members of the audience to go and handle them. And they do! Well, whatever turns you on...

It isn't my idea of fun so Carlos and I take a taxi to Raffles Hotel. It reminds me of the Ledra Palace Hotel in Nicosia, Cyprus. There are very few people about and we wander through the Lobby, past a huge open-air restaurant. No one dining. This erstwhile hub of international elitism is deserted, shabby and neglected. I am disappointed.

We wander on to the verandah and sit in the half light by the swimming pool. Palm trees reach beyond the roof tops. It's a still, calm night under the stars of Singapore and the ghosts are moving silently and sadly in Raffles Hotel. I understand it has since undergone much refurbishment to restore it to its former glory but it looks very sorry for itself tonight.

The next year when we docked at Singapore it poured with rain. I was busy all day as we had some very special passengers embarking. Crowds of people on the dockside waving banners and flags and creating quite a hullabaloo for the King and Queen of Malaysia and their entourage of about forty people. I didn't know that Malaysia had a King and Queen but this is what I discovered. The Malaysia Confederation of thirteen states hold an election every five years to determine who will become the Yang di-Pertuan Agong – 'King and Queen of Malaysia'. I always bring a copy of Debrett's Correct Form with me but I find no guidance in it for Malay royalty.

We have an Information List for the Royal Family and I soon track down Colonel Hew, aide-de-camp to His Majesty and my work is then much less fraught. But of course when the world cruise passengers get news that we have such illustrious passengers on board they all want to give special parties for the King and Queen and their family. We did the only thing possible – put all the requests to Colonel Hew.

The reply came back. Their Majesties would only accept one invitation – the one from our regular passenger, Mrs Louise Kirk Edwards from Tallahassee, Florida, known to the ship's company as

Lulu. She makes every World Cruise in *QE2* and books the same suite of rooms from year to year. She is such an anglophile. Her stateroom number is 1066!

She invites me to this small special party to be held midday in her stateroom. I can't find Colonel Hew to check protocol so I'm not sure whether I have to curtsy, bow, shake hands or whatever. By the time I arrive in the doorway it's too late. I didn't know the protocol. What to do?

The King and Queen are sitting in ordinary chairs at one side of the cabin. They wear casual clothes. Her Majesty is wearing an eau de Nil suit with a cerise blouse and carries a handbag over her left wrist. She is wearing tinted glasses. His Majesty is wearing a turquoise check safari suit. I approach, bow my head and shake hands with both of them.

Sitting on the bed is one of their daughters, Princess Norzhani, and I am invited to sit by her side. She is wearing a black skirt and a white silk long-sleeved over-blouse. She, too, is wearing tinted glasses. We have a long conversation. She speaks faultless English, loves London and shopping. Her son is at Eton.

There are various Ministers with their wives and a selection of passengers, the Captain and other officers with their wives. It is all very relaxed and just like any other party given by our well-loved and regular passenger, Lulu Edwards. But it *was* a 'one off' party, no doubt about it.

Eventually I go ashore with Angela, our Interpreter. The Landing Agent has given us information about the National Theatre on Clemenceau Avenue and assures us that we do not need to book tickets. Just go!

We hire a rickshaw. The man is like a stick insect, not an ounce of fat anywhere. Has anyone ever seen a fat rickshaw man? It's difficult to guess his age. All rickshaw men look alike. Lean, gaunt and smiling. He is eager for a fare and can see what he's going to pull – two medium-sized white women – off we go.

It's a strange experience. The rickshaw seems so small and flimsy and insecure. We can only just squeeze in. I feel guilty that this thin, little man should be pounding the streets of Singapore with two perfectly healthy women sitting like queens in his little sedan on wheels. I feel guilty that society permits such a form of transport. What will become of him when he is no longer strong enough to do this work? But then I argue with myself, what would the man do for a living if he didn't pull lazy white people in his rickshaw?

Riding in a rickshaw felt just a little bit like being royalty. Gazing on the crowds from our 'privileged' position, I'm sure if we had raised our hand in the royal wave they would have waved back!

He delivers us to the Theatre. The stage is under cover but the audience sits in the open air. We find a small booth under the trees and buy tickets from an excitable little man, then we have to find a seat, no seat number or row number – just find a seat. Any seat. It's an ocean of people, all talking at the same time. Such a din and such a crowd and so much excitement we get the giggles. What on earth are we doing here being pushed around in all this razzle-dazzle? We search for a place to sit and manage to squeeze into two seats near the end of a row. Call it mid-stalls.

The rippling acres of pale satin curtains part and the Chinese Opera begins. We can't understand a word of it and the noise is excruciating. I plug my ears with crumpled Kleenex tissue. It sounds like a thousand cats on hot tin roofs and a thousand broken violins and a thousand spoons being shaken in a thousand saucepans. We sit there mesmerised by the whole proceedings.

The Chinese actresses wear brilliantly coloured dresses of satin and brocade. We can't see their feet but they g l i d e across the stage as if they are on tiny wheels (probably are). Their hand movements are exquisite and obviously mean a lot to the story. I am intrigued by one actress wearing a gold embroidered gown of satin. She has an elaborate headdress decorated with the longest pheasant's feather I've ever seen. They don't grow to that length in Lincolnshire. It waves in a great arc beyond her head. At intervals, in anger or jest, she sweeps her hand across the feather and brings the tip of it down to her mouth. Then she releases it. The feather springs back and wafts in the air. She makes great play of this feather. It is obviously telling a lot. We sit in ignorance as the story unfolds. We listen to the 'music', experience the drama, the pulsating excitement of the audience all around us. Simply fascinating and I wouldn't have missed it for the world.

After the theatre we go to an open air restaurant to eat steamed crabs among other things and then take a rickshaw back to the ship. Getting into the habit now.

Later that evening Brian Price, Cruise Director and Bryan, Social Director, invite various friends and members of staff to join their shore party, including Joe and Mildred Loss. We are going to the famous or infamous Bugis Street. All crew members know about it but always seem reluctant to take a Lady Purser!

Bugis Street is a short street next to the open air food stalls. It has a tremendous buzz about it. There are sidewalk cafes, there are crowds and crowds of people wearing the most bizarre outfits meandering up and down, there is music, drinking and dancing.

We sit at a table on the sidewalk and order drinks. From time to time men and beautifully dressed women come to the table to laugh, joke and go on their way. It's all very frivolous. Then a most elegant woman pauses at our table. She is slim, shapely, beautifully made-up, shoulder length hair, low cut dress with a full skirt. Then, suddenly, she grabs her skirts, wafts them up to her face as if she were about to dance the cancan and lo and behold! She is not wearing panties. She, in fact, is a man! He loves the joke, smiles and flounces away.

It then dawns on me that most of the women wandering around are, in fact, men. After a brief study of this milling throng I realise that a good indicator as to gender is the size of the feet. But I can't tell Stork from butter in Bugis Street on this balmy spring night in Singapore.

Sri Lanka

Great excitement as we come alongside at Colombo. It is already hot and humid but, as usual, a large crowd is bustling about on the dockside, spotlessly clean with not a scrap of rubbish to be seen.

It is pulsating to the rhythm of a band of 24 men, some with drums, two of them with unusual horns like serpents and others with bells on a string, and they are producing the most stirring music. It's the famous Kandy drummers.

They are bare-chested wearing white headdresses like turbans, colourful beaded collars and white sarongs with broad red cummerbunds, no shoes or sandals. Gold bracelets flash in the morning sun. They give us a spectacular reception.

Bill Archibald, Manager of Thomas Cooks Tour Office on board, has an air-conditioned car at his disposal and invites me to join him. We have a hair-raising drive out of Colombo dodging buses and bullock carts, bicycles and Morris lorries.

Soon we are on our way to the Elephant Races driving through fertile country with rich vegetation. Many tea plantations. We go through Warakapola and Kegalle, a long, straggly town and the driver gets lost on a mountain road but we eventually find the elephants and the tourists, all wandering about amongst the trees.

The elephants are mountainous and have red soil on their ears. They grip a long palm leaf in their trunk, like a tight-rope walker's balancing pole. No one could tell me why the elephant needed this long leaf in its trunk. Passengers are riding the elephants. I keep my distance.

We drive on to Pinnawella to see the Elephant Orphanage where several dozen young animals, some only a few weeks old, are kept in parkland. Eight of them shuffle out of a long shed and into the park. Babies are fed 'baby milk' five times daily and are introduced to the herd once they've been checked. When they are big enough they work in the forests.

Elephant Races, Pinnawella, Sri Lanka

Eight baby elephant shuffle out of a shed and into the park

Sri Lanka has rich, plush valleys, wooded hills, massive bamboos, papaya, mango, bananas. Buffalo sleep under palm trees. Country people quietly go about their business. Children walk to the village shop, bigger boys push trolleys of firewood. Women are washing clothes in the river beds, men are working in the rice fields. One old man is tending a small patch of garden. Such calm, quiet, orderly people. They just stare and smile.

We pull up behind a crowd of people filling the road. It is a funeral party. All mourners are wearing white. A young man follows the coffin borne by six men scattering what looks like rice. Small white flags are stuck in the ground at intervals along the roadside.

The Sri Lankans have great respect for life and creatures. I watch a young boy, probably five or six years old, in a stream at the back of a rickety thatched hut. A buffalo stands on the bank and the boy is scooping water with his small hands and throws it on to the back of the buffalo. There are many dogs on the road and every vehicle stops or brakes to avoid hitting them.

During another visit to Sri Lanka I had time to see Colombo. It has managed to preserve the charm of the leisurely yesterdays and keeps its traditional bullock carts on the roads.

The Lighthouse Clock Tower, built in 1837 no longer performs a dual function but is probably the world's only lighthouse to be found in the middle of a city. Cinnamon Gardens is the exclusive residential district. Its name comes from the cinnamon plantation that once covered most of the area.

I didn't have time to linger in the National Museum but I learned that the original statue of the Goddess Tara is in our British Museum. Visitors gaze at a plaster cast. We really didn't seem to be able to keep our hands off anything!

Galle Face, once the Hyde Park of Colombo, is the city's largest open green, skirted by the sea along its length of nearly one mile. This is where the Colonial Army used to parade and race meetings were held here, too. Now families stroll and enjoy the sea breezes, meet their friends, walk their dogs and children fly their kites. And they come to watch the sun with its shades of gold and sepia sink into a mystical Indian Ocean.

We walk the mile in the searing heat of the midday sun. Only mad dogs and an English woman with Lou one of our Terrible Ten, would do such a thing... but we get to the end of the green and collapse in the Galle Face Hotel, built in 1864, the caravanserai of the British Empire. It remains stubbornly colonial – and still serving tea, thank goodness, but now probably totally made over for the twenty-first century.

Since my visit to Sri Lanka in the Eighties it has suffered much loss of life with the terrifying tsunami in 2005 and the political struggles for independence in the north of the island. I am lucky to have been able to record such unforgettable memories of these kindly people.

India

We sailed from Colombo in a thunderstorm, a phenomenon I never miss. My maternal grandfather, George Kirk, liked thunderstorms and would go out into the fields to stand and wonder as I did on the deck of the *QE2*. But at sea it is fantastic. Nothing but this vast expanse of night sky riven by jagged golden arrows flung into the sea from all angles and then the mighty explosions of thunder that echo across the dark ocean vault. Such power, such beautiful anger which prompts the question – Who do you think is in charge? Not the President of the United States!

I went on deck early for arrival Bombay (now Mumbai). There was the smell of incense in the wind and a thick sulphur pall hangs over the Gateway of India, built – yes, you've guessed it – to commemorate the visit of King George V and Queen Mary in 1911. It is styled on the 16th-century architecture of Gujarat.

In the dock area taking of photographs is prohibited. Large slogans are painted high on the walls. 'Discipline has improved our economy'; 'Don't be corrupted by rumours'; 'Corruption will be disciplined'.

I pick up a booklet which includes Tips for Tourist – 'Begging. You are likely to be accosted by street urchins. Please do not encourage begging and beware some of these may be pick-pockets.'

The Indian officials are anxious that passengers should not give to beggars. One of the officials tells me that the adult beggars have been bussed out of town for the duration of the stay of the *QE2*.

Another tip – 'Snake-charmers: This is an interesting experience and you will have to pay the snake-charmer about 50 cents or a dollar for the performance of the cobra and mongoose.'

Forewarned is forearmed and I took a taxi to the Taj Mahal Hotel not far from the waterfront as had so many of our passengers. It has marble floors, patios, fountains, shopping arcades. More of the same opulent luxury. Not for me, thank you!

From the hotel I wander into the back streets within spitting distance of the luxurious hotel. It's a shambles. Dirty, brown naked bodies asleep on the pavements. Thin children. Old men. Old women. Dogs eating dried excrement. Narrow streets.

Pavement dwellers stake out an area of about six feet by six feet and erect a roof of black plastic or cardboard or whatever they have. Muscle men living in adjoining tenements take over the pavement and intimidate the dwellers. They also take over the toilets and charge half a rupee for use. Women try to go only once a day, resulting in urinary diseases.

The streets bustle with black and yellow taxis weaving around red double-decker buses. Carts drawn by oxen seem oblivious of the mayhem. And people. People everywhere jostling on the crowded pavements.

There are many kiosks in the streets. One man has a tray of green leaves in front of him. He sprinkles ground red seeds on to a leaf, rolls it up and people buy the little leaf packet. The people chew these bright red seeds and then spit on to the pavement. I thought of the old lady in the hut in the foothills of Mount Kinabalu.

I find myself at a large building with carved balustrades and flimsy awnings on bamboo wooden frames. There is a spacious forecourt and beautifully maintained gardens. It looks like an Art Gallery or Museum.

The guard gets agitated when I start to take pictures. I apologise. Apparently it is the Municipal Building but I'm not sure why they should be 'censored'. The guard is a bit embarrassed but I leave quietly.

On to the Prince of Wales Museum and Art Gallery with an ornamented turret and dome and intricately carved archways and stonework. There are low box hedges round the garden plots. Tall palm trees stand sentinel.

Inside the building it is all very, very interesting. Don't skip this one. The paintings are small and meticulously executed. Many depict royal princesses and princes and their retinue. The blend of colours and detail are quite beautiful. One picture intrigues me. It is of two camels fighting (early 17th Century) – a popular sport at one time, it seems. Another picture 'Ladies playing Polo' – naked to the waist, if you please. (Early 18th Century)

On to the Museum section – human bone aprons (Nepal 18th Century) look like ivory lattice work on a band. I also see what I would describe as a stewpot. It is metal, circular with a lid. Guess! A Turban Box (16th Century). Rose water sprinklers look like elaborate vinegar bottles.

This Museum and Art Gallery is so very interesting and I am the only white visitor – crowded with Indians and their families.

In the middle of the traffic jam amongst the rubbish a huge black cow rests as peacefully as if it were in a meadow. It has large beige ears below its horns and it looks as if a bird is flying out of its head.

Back on board to the Queen's Room in time for an elegant Fashion Show. Beautiful Indian women are gliding across the floor with such poise, wearing gorgeous sarees. Purples, acid yellow, turquoise, green, gold. Pure silk and very expensive. In fact, they are wearing the same vivid colours as the girl prostitutes in the Cages. The difference is that the models sell the clothes, the girls in the Cages sell their bodies.

Crew members talk about the Cages and I had wanted to go there on previous trips but no one was willing to take me. But this year I get lucky. Two shipmates agree and we hire a taxi. The driver tells us to lock the door and keep the windows closed whilst we are in this area.

It is a row of terrace houses, three stories high, on either side of the street. The ground floor rooms have one wall knocked out and a metal mesh gate, rather like the old-fashioned hand-operated lifts we used to have. This folding gate is across the wall flush with the street. A cage. There are four or five young girls in each ground floor 'cage'. They press close to the grill, eyeing the shambles in the street with apathy, their nubile bodies swathed in brilliantly coloured sarees, like gaudy butterflies at a window pane. Some are smiling at us gawking at them.

All are waiting for a customer. Or is it a client? I don't know. I'm in uncharted waters now. I raise my camera to take a picture but they cover their faces. There are older women, too, worn out with the ravages of the life they lead and I wonder how on earth they can compete with these young girls.

Upstairs the windows are open with shabby curtains flapping in the breeze. These are the rooms the girls use when 'booked'. The average life expectancy of the girl prostitutes is thirty-three. The driver tells us that many girls are from distant villages. Their parents sell them so that they can come to the city for work. At the end of this street, next to the Cages is a Dentist, a Doctor, a Food Clinic and a sign which says, 'Abortions 64 rupees'.

Outside the Cages the street is littered with human debris. Bundles of people lying in the gutter, some are sleeping on thin mattresses, some on the ground, some smoking, some gambling.

The maimed and mutilated bodies of the dusty children look like middle-aged dwarfs. One child on all fours has wheels strapped to his knee stubs. At least he is mobile, unlike many adults who are slumped

Prostitutes at The Cages, Bombay, India

in a heap, sleeping and dreaming perhaps, in the clouds of hashish – and who can blame them for escaping the reality of that life.

Goats, bullocks, mangy cats and dogs wander about. Squalor, depravity, indignity, starvation. Life here has no value and the girls cannot even know this because they can compare it with nothing in their sphere.

Drive on chauffeur, enough. Now we can wind down the windows again but the sickening sweet and sour stench of rotting fruit, rotting bodies and excrement is appalling. But we are safe. The starving children won't throw themselves into the cab to steal our expensive cameras, rings, watches or purses...

Since my world cruises everything has moved on a pace, a pace more depraved. Over the years it has become a growth area, market forces have taken over and now jet planes are fully-booked with sex holidaymakers from Europe to the Far East. Consenting adults can do it from the top of a flagpole for all I care but to abuse helpless children...

The driver has stopped and from a wall we gaze down on a huge compound of stone troughs, row upon row, with a stone trench running through the centre. There are single storey buildings on both sides. Many people are bent over the troughs washing clothes. This is an open air wash-house and people come here to have a communal wash day.

We move on and the driver pulls up at open double gates. Begging children bombard us for 'one dollar'. They are thin and shabby and look so old with their lined, pinched faces and dull eyes.

We walk through the gates. On the left is a storage shed full of logs, neatly sawn, piled to the roof. On the right is a big open yard and spaced at intervals of about six feet I count four piles of burning wood, the pungent smoke rising and filling the air with a mixture of incense and wood – and something else? Human flesh.

These are funeral pyres. Groups of men stand around at a respectable distance. I catch a glimpse of white in the wood pile. The shroud. I wonder if it is a thirty-year-old prostitute's body.

The visit to Bombay moved me deeply. The splendour of the luxury hotels, the squalor of the back streets, the pity of the Cages, the child on knee wheels, the ostentatious glamour of the Fashion Show and the priceless silk sarees displayed. The huge divide between rich and poor. And the help from international charities is not always sensible. Bras are sent to the poor who cut them in half and use them as rice bowls!

China

China – in friendship

Working non-stop since New York with the frantic embarkations and disembarkations at so many ports we all breathe a huge sigh of relief when *QE2* sails into Hong Kong harbour.

Not only is Hong Kong one of our most exciting ports of call, it is the longest stop-over during the World Cruise. We stay four or five days and some passengers take overland tours and rejoin the ship in Japan. The rest of the ship's company have a chance to loosen up, shop, sightsee and sleep.

As we ease into Kowloon harbour we pass over the graveyard of our beloved RMS *Queen Elizabeth*.

Cunard's flag-ship was sold to a Taiwanese shipping magnate, C. Y. Tung, head of the C. Y. Tung Shipping Group of Hong Kong in 1970. He was planning to convert it to a floating university and learning centre and RMS *Queen Elizabeth* was renamed *Seawise University.*

She sank here on 9 January 1972 after burning for fourteen hours following a fire which began near the stern and swept inexplicably through her. Inexplicable because there are fire sprinklers (alarms) fitted into all deckheads of this eighty thousand ton vessel. They activate immediately there is a fire. There was no loss of life but it was a catastrophic end to such a celebrated liner.

We are about halfway round the world and my eighty-day week is beginning to tell. I am exhausted. A flight from the UK brings in the replacement catering and other staff. They tramp thousands of miles with laden silver trays on their shoulders, pandering to every whim of the passengers and they are ready for some well-earned leave. But most of the ship's company stay with the *QE2* for the complete eighty-day World Cruise. It's a long haul but it has many rewards.

I eventually go down the gangway with some shipmates to get away from it all for a while and we decide to take a Chinese junk to Aberdeen. We are going to need every ounce of energy for the overland to Canton.

The harbour is swarming with river craft of all sorts and sizes from flimsy little vessels that could be blown away by a puff of wind, to gigantic container ships. A tug crosses our bows. Painted in large letters along the side are the words 'Pollution Control'. We pass close by the shore where shacks cling precariously to rocks. Goodness knows why they don't topple into the water.

Aberdeen is Hong Kong's main fishing village and hundreds and hundreds of people live on their junks and sampans – large, medium and small. Many are motorised. Some are floating delicatessens and go from boat to boat selling food. Women captain the vessels, steering with a pole. They seem to have the muscles of a navvy in negotiating the waterways. Many of the younger women have a baby strapped to their back. We have a lengthy lunch at the floating restaurant – a richly decorated Chinese Palace with lots of red lanterns – and meet Officers from the *Canberra* who are also getting away from it all.

Kwangchow (Canton) – The City of Five Rams

Ports of call for the World Cruises are planned at least one year ahead. Cunard Superintendents visit the Port Authorities around the world to check on the tides, harbours, docking and all facilities needed for bringing a ship alongside. Other representatives visit the Ministries, the Tourist Offices and organisations concerned with tourism to stream-line arrangements for sightseeing – availability of coaches, restaurants.

This year Cunard is breaking new ground and we are taking hundreds of World Cruise passengers on a three-day excursion to mainland China to visit Kwangchow (Canton). It is February 1977.

We have a staff briefing to end all briefing sessions. Pay attention

Welcome to Canton, China – crowds of people stare in amazement.

please. China is a new challenge with specific rules and regulations for admitting Western tourists. A 'blanket' visa for all passengers has been successfully negotiated and the rules were laid down twelve months before our proposed visit.

Our passengers must be divided into groups of twenty-five people. Each group must be led by a Cunard Officer/Official and no passenger will be allowed to change groups once allocated and documented. Passengers must do what they are told by the China Tour Guide. If a passenger doesn't want to go on any of the organised sightseeing tours then he/she must stay in the hotel.

One American passenger pulls his bottom lip aside and says, 'Ah, gee, no problem. We'll just take a cab for a ride...'

'But, sir, there are no taxis and there are no street signs.'

I am to lead a group of twenty Spanish-speaking passengers. All the information is in English so after my official duties I am ensconced in my cabin translating the information for them.

After our briefing there is a rehearsal for passengers to find Group locations and meet their Group Leader. Passengers are given name tags, currency and Customs forms. Everything has to be said at least twice to be absolutely certain that passengers know and understand the situation. I still have an irritating tendency to say everything twice! The Chinese are very punctilious and we must follow the programme to the letter and minute.

Next morning I am up at 5 o'clock to collect passports from the China Desk and then I go to the allotted Group Station to check my passengers and give out passports and vaccination certificates. At six thirty I march my party down the gangway leaving the Group Number placard at the Security Office to prove that we are off the ship.

After walking fifty yards (note the precision) we are met by the China Tour Guide who escorts us to a bus which takes us to Hong Kong station and we file on to the special train. I do a quick head count again and the train is on its way. It's only seven o'clock in the morning but it feels like lunchtime and I'm hungry.

The journey to the border takes one and a half hours through the New Territories past shacks and small houses, building sites with flimsy scaffolding. Farm land and rice paddies. We arrive at the Chinese border on the Shumchun River. The Guide instructs us to leave the train and go to the Hong Kong Departure Immigration. This Guide then leaves us.

My Chinese Guide is a smiling young man speaking fluent English and Spanish. His diction is Castilian.

'You must have studied in Madrid,' I say.

'No.' He's shy and turns away.

'But your accent is so pure.'

'Thank you,' he smiles. 'I have never left China.'

There are crowds of people at the frontier, their eyes riveted on 'the invaders' and we stare back as we march across the bridge. A soldier is taking a photo of us. A large notice in Chinese and English states 'Long Live the People's Republic of China'. We have arrived.

The train is huge and pompous and hissing steam impatiently. Very imperial with a wide centre corridor. Each passenger has an upholstered wing chair on a swivel so that he/she can look directly out of the window. A picnic lunch is served with scented tea, but there is no sugar.

We are soon gazing at lots of small boats and junks floating along lakes with mountains as a back drop. Rice paddies look like water-logged meadows. Men and women wearing broad-brimmed coolie hats are working the soil with hoes and rakes. Children are collecting wood. Others are leading water buffalo on a rope. Since leaving Bombay, Sri Lanka, Singapore, Bali I have noticed that everyone, young and old, is working.

The train stops at various stations and locals get on and off. Men and women wear navy blue or grey baggy pyjama suits and mules or light canvas shoes. They are laden down with a wooden yoke balancing panniers, watering cans, baskets, or bundles. They have developed a sort of trot – perhaps it eases the strain on their shoulders. I can see no farm machinery. Water buffalo do the work. Every scrap of land seems to be fertile. Along the railway track there are small patches of cabbages and other green vegetables and beyond, for as far as the eye can see, land under cultivation.

During the journey I distribute hotel room numbers to my passengers explaining the currency and Customs procedure. I have to emphasise that there is no tipping in China!

We chug into Canton Station. A cathedral of a place. We are decanted from the trains and pour into buses for the drive to our Hotel – Luxinshan (Tung Fang) watched by crowds and crowds of people staring in amazement at this bizarre sight before their eyes.

Tung Fang is an enormous hostelry of eleven stories with 1,233 rooms. There is no central heating. My room is spacious and cold with green walls and two beds, both with canopies. A Chinese version of the Victorian four-poster. A desk with stationery and several chairs.

On the table is a teapot and tea service with tea, a thermos of hot water and a bowl of oranges. Passengers are requested not to remove anything from the hotel rooms. For example, the teapot! There are attendants on each floor, two ladies sitting at a small table at the end of the corridor, eager to be of assistance whenever needed.

Our first excursion is to the Children's Palace. This is where children study and play close to the factory where their parents work. Children with painted faces wear pink, scarlet, and blue and are carrying wreaths and arches of yellow flowers. We see an open air display of gymnastics by the children. They perform on rush mats and are as light as feathers with their leaps and somersaults. All wear light trousers and bright sweaters of various colours, contrasting sharply with the adults who wear dark blue or grey. Some displays are like Kung Fu – others more like ballet. Children line our path as we wander to the next display. They all wave red pompoms and applaud us!

In this room children are doing the most beautiful paintings from top to bottom of the paper or was it from the bottom to the top? Finally we go into a room set up theatre-style and see the most

Welcome to the Children's Palace

enchanting show of singing and dancing by children, aged between seven and thirteen I would guess. They look like dolls with their rouged cheeks and scarlet lips. Such confidence and such capriciousness! They are gorgeous. One boy, about eight years old, sings solo. All about Chairman Mao apparently. A complete orchestra of musicians – girls and boys – close the show.

The girls are wearing skirts and have very white legs. Probably because they usually wear trousers – no suntan. Yesterday and today I notice several children with casts in their eyes. And they like to hold hands, the human touch. I get the feeling that they need to be cuddled a bit more

This evening we attend a banquet. The table groans with all the dishes. We have two Chinese guests at our table. A whole congratulatory experience of friendship as Chinese officials and Cunard officials jump to their feet offering toasts as chairs squeaked and squawked on bare floors.

The next morning we make another early start. Mr Gurson, the First Secretary from the British Embassy in Peking joins my group today. We drive through the wide, deserted streets into the country to visit the Pingchow People's Commune, Nanhai County.

This Commune has 287 production teams with 69,100 people living in 16,700 families. It cultivates 4,563 hectares of farmland producing mainly rice with sugar cane, vegetables and fruits. It also raises pigs, dairy cows, poultry and fish. The scale of the project is mind-boggling.

But everything is so primitive. For instance, I spot a young man on a steep canal bank with a bucket. He is filling it with a small wooden ladle on a long pole. Pigs wander about among the broken-down buildings. Chickens scratch about for anything edible. All buildings are shabby and badly in need of paint.

We are taken into a large room like a barn and sit at a long table. Tea and cigarettes are served then the Chief of the Commune gives a talk about the work. Communes have their own primary and secondary schools. The Chinese are very proud of their achievements and wish to make a good impression. The talk lasts for about half an hour followed by a discussion period. Then we are divided into groups of seven to visit a private home. My group is directed to a small dwelling where a man lives with six children, four sons, two daughters, one of whom is still studying. The house is clean but sparsely furnished. The welcome is warm and the etiquette faultless.

Next we go to a hospital. The floors are filthy. Some patients are on stretchers. Others are sitting on benches in a corridor, waiting to be seen by a doctor. Herbs are used a lot in treatments.

We have lunch at the Commune and, of course, we all need the ladies room. I make enquiries and with some trepidation invite the ladies to follow me along a footpath under the trees and there we are in front of a small, wooden building, looking and smelling like a cow shed. It is gloomy inside and we have to squat over holes in the floor. There is room for about four people at a time. I get the giggles at the sight of these affluent American ladies, hair perfectly coiffured, their hands meticulously manicured, struggling to keep their balance as they squat over an earth closet with their knickers round their ankles.

Finally the Zoological Park. Two pandas in a large fenced area look very fed up. They are quite big and fat, sitting on their bums peeling bamboo. I am surprised how dirty their white coats are! The bamboo trees are very tall with a lot of foliage.

Back to the hotel for a brief respite. I long to put everything on hold so that I can digest the scenes and sights and sounds but there is no let-up with our hectic itinerary and it is theatre after dinner. It is so big, everything in China seems huge – the sky, the rivers, the halls, the barns, the railway station, the hotel – enormous.

An ocean of ice blue satin curtains ripple in front of the stage. The commere is a young woman in a pale-blue tailored suit, white shoes. Very smart. First, a Chinese Orchestra of drums and gongs give a rousing performance then a colourful dance by young men and women giving thanks for the rubber production; another one gives thanks for the electric light produced on the completion of the hydro-electric scheme. Chairman Mao is always acknowledged and thanked. Vocalists, male and female, and then the most impressive piece of the evening.

It depicts the struggle of 1935 (Chiang Kai-chek) and the battle for the Chain Bridge. The bridge is a massive piece of heavy scenery filling the stage and there is something of the Chinese resilience in this huge bridge and the people fighting on it. Superb dancing by 24 males. Quite, quite stunning.

The next morning we have yet another early start to visit the Tahsin Ivory Handicraft Factory twelve miles from Canton on the Pearl River Delta. It is positively Dickensian. Five hundred and seventy workers, 40 per cent women, sit at benches with very poor light working on intricate ivory carvings. Some men are working on the famous ivory balls within balls, their feet manipulating two planks of wood, rather like pedalling a sewing machine. This causes the piece of ivory on which they are working to revolve. The ivory ball has 40 free-moving concentric layers. The smallest product of the factory is the size of a grain of rice!

The oldest men are doing the finest filigree work – more experienced? But it is all so dark and dismal and the workers sit in front of blank walls. They probably don't notice them because they are bent over their work engrossed in the complex designs. All personnel take part in the creation and design of the items.

After leaving the ivory factory we are taken on a drive around Canton. It is a spacious city with broad tree-lined avenues. No traffic – just bikes and an occasional lorry or bus. No shops. Dozens and dozens of people stop to stare at us – and no wonder!

On to Pan Shi Restaurant on a lake where we have another banquet to end our visit to mainland China. Three hours later, speeches and good wishes reinforced, we leave for the station where huge crowds of people wait for us.

After departure from Canton each Group Leader must collect the passports from the passengers. This is vitally important. The first thing I must do on return to the ship is to hand these passports to the China Tour Office. The ship will not be allowed to sail until all passports have been checked. But not all the passengers on the tour are rejoining the ship. They are what we call 'finally landing' in Hong Kong so they must keep their passports. And then some of the passengers on the tour are joining the ship for the first time in Hong Kong. Another set of documentation for them. And we have to get it right!

We arrive Hong Kong at five o'clock in the evening with no missing passengers, no sick passengers, no one has lost their passport and no one has been robbed. On the contrary, during the train journey back to Hong Kong one of the Chinese Guides, an attractive young lady, comes through the train with a bag full of items. These things had been thrown into the waste paper bins in the various hotel rooms. So armed with the name and room number of each passenger this Guide returns all the discarded items to their owners – including a pair of laddered tights!

As the lights of Hong Kong come into view I reflect on the tranquillity and space in mainland China. Time stands still but soon the cacophony of busy Hong Kong blots out that peace.

It has been a unique experience meeting the kindly Chinese people with their exquisite manners and courtesy, their desire to please, their lovely wide-eyed children. The venture has been a great success and went without a hitch thanks to the excellent organisation by the Chinese officials. Efficient and smiling.

So I climb the gangway of the *QE2*, exhilarated at having visited one of the most interesting countries in the world. I take the passports to the China Tour Office and then make a beeline for my cabin, kick off my shoes and collapse with a stiff drink!

South Lantau

We embark a lot of passengers in Hong Kong and there will be a

Captain's Reception immediately after sailing but I do not have the final number of passengers so cannot finish the invitations.

Last year I did some research and discovered that it's possible to stay overnight at a Buddhist Monastery on South Lantau island. The information is tucked away in a leaflet I picked up at the Hong Kong Tourist Information Office. I want to go there and the leaflet suggests writing or telephoning for accommodation so I find a phone booth on the dock. A Chinese workman helps me with the coins and I dial the number. There is a crackle and a splutter and a squeak and then I hear a man's voice. He seems far, far away. His voice is breaking up as it comes down the line and I can't understand a word he's saying.

'Good morning. Do you speak English?' I ask.

'Yes.'

'Could I book a single room with facilities for tomorrow night please?'

'Yes,' there was a pause and then 'that is good. Name please?'

And that was all there was to it. I put the phone down and took a deep breath. What on earth was I thinking of? Sleeping in a Monastery on top of a mountain on an island, miles away from the ship. What is more I hadn't asked the rate for the room! These mini-terrors often sweep through me after I've made a reckless decision so I am accustomed to this dose of folly. I knew it would pass and it did.

When you travel alone you learn to read faces, follow their eyes to see what they are looking at – your bag, your body. Decide about the smile, if there is one. Watch the way a person moves, the body language. Be alert. Keep your wits about you. Never tell about dangerous situations and don't depend on anyone. Fortunately I have a good sense of direction and can find my way around. Buddhists are right in their belief that expectation is one of the great sources of suffering. Think about it.

But I need to know a little more about this island so I walk into the Royal Hong Kong Police Station not far from the Peninsular Hotel. It is a small office with a high counter. Two very smart members of the Royal Hong Kong Police face me. They are wearing blinding white shirts with gold on their epaulettes. I present my passport and my landing card.

'I would like to visit South Lantau and stay the night. Is it tranquil?' I use this phrase everywhere in the world and it is generally understood. Are there bandits? muggers? robbers? murderers?

Their eyes glaze over.

'You go alone?' One of the officers stood back from the high counter, head back, mouth open.

'Yes.'

He stares at the other officer and then disappears through a door at the back of the office as if I had insulted him, leaving his colleague stuck with me. At that moment another police officer comes through that same door. He is wearing a lot more gold pips on his epaulettes.

He fixes his eyes on me.

'We cannot guarantee anyone's safety.' He purses his lips and he, too, steps away from the counter.

'Of course not.' I held his gaze. 'I'm not asking for a guarantee of safety. Could I go there and walk about in broad daylight?'

'There are bandits in the mountains. And a lot of building work taking place on the island.' His dark eyes flash in fear. I recognised the same flash of fear on the face of the police officer in the Police Station in Arica, Peru when I was making plans for a similar 'folly'.

'I've phoned the Monastery and they have accommodation.'

'You will be safe in the Monastery.' He half-turns, dismissing me. 'Do not stay in any boarding house or private accommodation,' and disappears back to his office.

I then reconnoitre my escape route for tomorrow. Leaving the Police Station I find the quay where I will take the ferry and discover that the boat calls at several islands. So I copy the name of my island and the name of my disembarkation town – Mui Wo – on to a postcard. Then back to the ship to prepare an overnight bag and it hits me. The irresponsibility of what I plan to do. No one would have any idea where to look for me. So I write a note and take it to the office, tucking the sealed envelope under the edge of the blotter on my desk.

The next morning I am up and away at crack of dawn for the seven o'clock ferry. We cast off and wheedle our way between the sampans and junks in the harbour and soon have nothing but sea around us. The boat arrives at one island after another. At each call passengers pour down the gangway and more passengers scramble on board with their bags of oranges, live chickens, bunches of silver fish dangling from long poles, bundles of vegetables and bags.

What a good thing I have the name of the island clearly printed! I have no idea where to get off so as we arrive at each island I sidle up to the Chinese Bo'sun at the gangway and flash my card under his nose. Each time he shakes his head. No, not this one.

Here I am out on the briny and beginning to wonder if this place exists. I am still haunting him as we arrive at the fourth island. This time he nods. I go down the gangway at Mui Wo (Silvermine Bay). It gets its name from the actual silver mines now sealed and boarded up near Pak Ngan Heung. In front of me is the bus I want – to Po Lin Tse (Ngong Ping) – 'The Precious Lotus Monastery'.

I climb aboard and join Chinese ladies carrying baskets of oranges and packages. There are a few men. Everyone is on the move whether they are in London or South Lantau.

We follow the gentle undulations of the South Lantau Road for some time and I see many new buildings and roads under construction – that Police Inspector had been right. We climb higher and higher into thickly wooded hillsides with deep ravines and valleys below. Soon we are on a single track with the bright green branches of the bushes and trees teasing the windows of the bus. The track is so narrow there are only a few passing places for oncoming traffic.

After about forty minutes we pull off the road into a large, deserted car park completely surrounded by trees and dense shrubs. The only vehicle there is a minibus. The track is now too steep and winding for the bigger bus so we have to transfer. I follow the Chinese

One small courtyard is divided by a grey stone wall from which a complete circle has been shaped, Po Lin Monastery.

people into the minibus and we are on our way again, labouring up the winding, mountainous track. Then it bumps to a halt in swirling mist. We have arrived. It has taken almost an hour from Mui Wo.

The Chinese passengers know exactly what they are about and are gone. They just evaporated in the swirling mist. The minibus disappears and I stand there alone in this ghostly haze, like Orphan Annie, with my bag at my feet. Just for one horrible, terrifying moment I am gripped with a steely, cold fear. The silence and the mist are scary. Nothing seems real any more. Then the mist clears and I see the Temple Gate. It is a huge triple arch in stone, highly decorated with carvings and gold lettering and sculptures, half human, half animal, at the base.

I wander under the arch into a wide forecourt. In the centre is a circular garden, brilliant with red and pink and cerise flowers. Beyond it is a broad flight of steps leading to a Temple. I walk straight ahead and up the flight of steps flanked by stone banisters. At the top of the steps, outside the temple, large red lanterns are suspended between a row of smooth, red pillars. Carved balustrades in stone protect the balcony and there are flowers in tubs everywhere. This is one of my enduring memories of the Monastery – such a profusion of flowers and perfume and colour.

The doors of the Temple are wide open. I am not a Buddhist and do not know the protocol but I put my bag down and step just inside the open entrance doors and stare. Opposite me, on the other side of the Temple, about fifty yards away, a golden Buddha smiles down from a golden dais. It is awesome to be alone with such a deity. I stare for quite a long time. At him. At the decor. To the right is a row of blue and white urns and more golden figures. To the left of the Buddha is a huge carved lion in bronze. The beams and joists of the ceiling are decorated in gold and red with birds and animals. The walls are intricately carved and painted in red and gold. Bright red lanterns hang all around. Everywhere the smell of burning incense adds to the mystery, to the richness yet simplicity of it all. Time stands still.

Feeling somewhat humbled I go back down the steps and wander along the side of the Temple into a courtyard. The mist obscures everything like a gentle grey curtain of chiffon then it lifts to give tantalising glimpses of red and gold temples and red and gold buildings with dramatic views of the deep gorges and valleys beyond.

I stand in the courtyard trying to get my bearings in this beautiful, silent world shrouded with mist. I have no idea where to 'check in'. There must be a reception office somewhere but I feel quite disorientated. Then I see a thin little man shuffling across the courtyard.

'Excuse me. Reception. Where is it please?'

'This way,' and he directs me to a red building opposite the Temple.

A wizened man of middle age is at a desk in a dusty little office. It is bare and stark but he welcomes me warmly in precise English and asks me to sign the register. There are two, side by side, on a table. One in Chinese, one in English. It is the size of a Victorian family Bible. I am asked to pay my bill (HK$30) which includes all meals. He tells me the meal hours three times so obviously diners must be punctual. Breakfast 8 o'clock, lunch 12.30, supper 5.30.

I am then shown to 'my room' by a skinny, energetic man who has appeared from nowhere. He is as agile as a monkey as he scrambles up a dark, damp, concrete stairway at the side of the building and I follow him through a door on the left and we are in a passage with windows. The rooms are on one side, partitioned by plywood screens, overhead is a loft. I am taken into a room with six wooden trestle tables against the walls, leaving the centre of the room clear. The floor is bare. On each table is a raffia mat, one blanket and an eiderdown less than two inches thick.

Surrounding each bed is a net curtain. Why? It can't be for mosquitoes – it's too cold. My eyes sweep around this sparse, cheerless room. From the one and only window I look down on the courtyard below. This is my single room with facilities!

I leave my room to go and explore. At the end of the passage there is an altar. Someone has placed a bowl of oranges on it. Candles flicker and incense burns.

I wander all around the grounds. One small courtyard is divided by a grey stone wall in the centre of which a complete circle has been beautifully cut and shaped to give access to the next courtyard.

At every turn there are secluded courtyards adorned with tubs of freesias along the walls and outside the doors, all sheltered by trees with tall, smooth, silvery trunks.

Alleyways and steps separate the various buildings and outhouses. Near the kitchen area is a building with a wooden bridge consisting of a flight of steps on either side leading to a small balcony. The 'bridge' looks like the famous Monet Bridge at Giverny without the water and it stands flush with the building. Underneath the 'bridge' is a bench and desk – it is an office with no door, open to the courtyard.

Women are washing clothes at stone troughs, some are sitting on stools preparing vegetables, others are working in the vegetable garden. I say women but I cannot tell whether they are women or men.

There are a lot of dogs prowling about, mainly Chows but there are some of the Heinz variety, sniffing around the freesia tubs and fighting each other. There must have been more than two dozen of them. I sit on a low wall under a tree and watch. The fight begins when a dog from the kitchen area trespasses into a courtyard, or vice versa. Territorial imperative.

It is soon time for lunch. The Refectory is a large barn with windows. It is huge and cold and accommodates more than 200 people. The doors are left open. High above, sparrows and swallows flutter and swoop under the rafters.

Just inside the door a little fat man (Restaurant Manager?) sits at a small desk and tells me to go to Table 6. Tables are circular and we sit on stools. I think the other diners were staff from the Monastery. I am joined by an intense young Frenchman who is on holiday. He is doing research on fish farming in Japan so I learn a bit more about fugu fish.

Lunch is good but it takes me a long time to eat. Every Chinese eye is on me as I struggle with the chopsticks. I forgot to bring a spoon! I'm not sure what I am eating but recognised mushrooms, greens and celery. All the food is vegetarian and every meal is the same. On a table in the centre of the room is a large wooden barrel full of boiled rice. Just help yourself to more. It is still steaming hot when I leave an hour later.

I go up the hill towards Lantau Peak at the back of the Monastery. It is 3000 feet high, the second highest peak in the whole of Hong Kong. By now the sun has dispersed the clouds and I can see the Monastery and grounds below for the first time. There are many buildings clustered around the Temple, iridescent almost with its decorated terra cotta roof contrasting with the grey stone walls around the many courtyards. The gold, the scarlet lanterns on the balconies, the profusion of flowers and the trees. It looks like a film set.

Clearly defined footpaths snake their way from the Monastery across the mountains in all directions. The smell of wood smoke and burning incense drifts in the air. It all seems so unreal. So peaceful. There is a stillness, a calm difficult to describe but wonderful to behold.

I come across the Tea Plantation. It is the only one in Hong Kong apparently. A small tea processing factory and a little tea house have been built behind the main temple and 'tea with a mountain flavour' can be sampled and packets bought.

Along a footpath beyond the plantation I find stables with eight horses. A group of young Chinese horsemen in a paddock near the mounting block are taking it in turns to ride an enormous horse. I stand some distance away, at the back of them, and I don't think they can see me.

They are the most handsome Chinese I have seen. Their thick black hair is cut in the style of a mediaeval page boy. They are wearing dark red sweaters, white riding breeches and black leather knee boots. They have beautiful bodies. Strong, straight backs, smooth, muscular thighs. Very sensuous.

Most of the Chinese I have met are thin and work-weary because they toil such endless hours but these young men are outrageously handsome, almost arrogant – and they ride with great panache. I decide they must be from Hong Kong Chinese High Society, possibly a polo team.

When I get back to the Monastery I find people, young and old, milling around. Day trippers! And the teenagers have transistor radios with them. Switched on! I groan inwardly but the trippers didn't stay long and peace descends again.

I sit on a low wall under a tree to listen to the monks and nuns at prayer. They are in the small temple just across the courtyard. Large square iron lamps are suspended outside the temple. They look like our Victorian street lights. The doors of the temple are open and I can see the monks processing. They chant in a fast rhythm to the accompaniment of drum beats. They wear grey most of the time but during afternoon prayers the monks' robes are brown.

A young monk comes to sit on the wall next to me. He is very tall and thin and the bristle on his bare head is quite blond. He has good, square-cut features. His eyes are blue and far-seeing but he looks ill.

'Hello, my name's Andrew,' and he continues to trace a carving on to tissue paper. 'I'm from New Zealand.'

'A long way from home,' I say.

'Yes. I enlisted for the Vietnam War and soon decided that I wanted no more truck with Killer Man. Much to my parents' chagrin I left New Zealand to become a monk. I was a novice in Thailand.' He pauses and stares across the courtyard. 'And so here I am... but I have to go back to New Zealand for an operation.'

'Oh, I'm so sorry.'

'I'm having trouble with my back and need surgery.' He pauses again.

Apparently this new lifestyle, the long hours of meditation and unusual postures are causing problems. I watch as he folds the tissue paper carefully and then gets up. He is very tall.

'I'm going now.'

'Oh, you don't live here, then?'

'No, I'm staying at a Hermitage over the mountain. Goodbye,' and he strode away to find one of those concrete footpaths.

'Good luck, Andrew.'

After supper I decide to walk to a small summit half a mile from the monastery. I want to see what is on the other side but cloud envelops me. I don't linger and return to the Monastery immediately.

At 7.15 p.m. we all get ready for bed. 'We' being three other ladies who have come into 'my room'. I recognise them. They were on the minibus. Male and female guests at the Monastery are segregated and their husbands are accommodated in a separate room. All are Chinese, one is quite elderly, but I find it difficult to assess their ages.

They show me how to make my bed on the table. First, the

blanket on top of the raffia mat, then you get into the padded eider-down, not unlike a sleeping bag. I put the other blanket and my coat on top. My handbag is on a table next to the bed and I placed my small travel bag on the floor underneath.

The Chinese women signal to me to put both bags on the table inside the curtain. I mimed that they would be all right but they insist that I put everything inside the curtain with me. Handbag, travel bag. I lay on the hard bed table wondering why nothing could be left on the floor. Thieves? There couldn't be thieves in this peaceful, non-materialistic world. Rats perhaps...

The Chinese ladies are wearing trousers and quilted jackets and slept in them. Sensible. I undress and put on a pale blue nylon nightdress and matching negligée. Could anyone have been so stupid? I knew the Monastery was at the top of a mountain but I didn't know that I would sleep on a raffia mat on a table. I am frozen stiff! I pull on two pairs of tights and get myself into all the clothes I have brought with me, nicked a blanket from another table and lay down. There is one fluorescent electric light in the room but when the ladies switched it off a candle burned all night and I could smell incense too.

The bed table is very uncomfortable. I try all kinds of thoughts but the table remains hard and I remain restless and cold. And as I lay there I thought of many things and I thought of Alexander Solzhenitsyn. I imagine the room would be much the same as those he describes in the prison camps except that they would be much more crowded and noisy – and dirty and horrible. The prisoners used to sleep in their clothes. And the other thing that reminded me of him was the statement in one of his books – 'Do not pursue what is illusory – property and position: all that is gained at the expense of your nerves decade after decade, and is confiscated in one fell night.' These monks and nuns had willingly given up all pursuit of position and property.

My Chinese friends have a restless night, too. They are standing in a huddled group in the middle of the room, chatting quietly. One of them, the elderly one, is smoking. It doesn't smell like Western tobacco. I must have drifted into sleep because suddenly I am awakened by a booming, hollow, sound. It is very, very loud and slow and rhythmic, echoing through the buildings and courtyards and across the mountains. It is someone beating a gong, a huge gong to give that resonance.

I go to the window and look down on to the courtyard below but can see no one – it's too dark. The booming eventually stops. The silence is enormous and I lay awake until the blackness fades and dawn comes.

The sound of that gong in the blackness of the night stays with me, echoing across my memory. It is comforting. I don't know why. At this very moment, in Po Lin Monastery the same gong will be beaten, the same prayers will be chanted and the dogs will be fighting. There is something appealing about a life style that can endure through the ages. Unchanged. Untainted.

I am mobile by quarter past seven. The Chinese ladies have rolled up their covers and gone. Later I saw them visiting shrines set back from little footpaths among the bushes.

Next to our room there is a flush toilet, no toilet paper. In the passage is a stone trough with a Victorian-style wash bowl and a cold water tap. This is where I wash – shivering with cold. The waste water is tipped into the trough and runs away along drains around the outside wall. A zinc bath is suspended on a nail. Ready for bath night? I grew icicles at the very thought of it. My ablutions complete I am surprised to hear a voice. A woman near the little altar at the end of the passage is reading aloud, slowly.

After breakfast I make my way through the Tea Plantation to walk along a mountain footpath winding through bracken and thick bushes. The path dips and curves between gentle little hills rising to steeper ones, reminiscent of the Scottish Highlands. But the concrete path intrigues me. Miles and miles and miles of well-made, permanent concrete paths meandering across these mountains.

Ahead I can see an archway. It is like a door frame without a door, standing on this footpath in the middle of nowhere. It is dedicated to a monk and bears a Chinese inscription and in English underneath it says: 'There is no time – what is memory?'

Coming towards me is a Chinese woman. She is carrying two big string net bags full of packages and vegetables dangling from each end of a pole across her shoulders. Then I understand why there is a permanent concrete path. The path is the only means of getting across the mountains so it would need to be passable in all weathers.

I produce my camera, hold my head on one side and smile. She stops and nods and smiles for my photo. The remarkable thing I notice about this lady is that she is not wearing trousers. She's wearing a navy blue skirt and jacket. It's the first time I have seen a pair of adult bare Chinese legs. I watch her disappear with her lolloping gait synchronised to manage her heavy burden.

You will remember that I discovered this Monastery in a little Information leaflet. Well, tucked away in another corner of that leaflet was 'Advice on Snakes'. Apparently quite a lot of snakes can be found on Lantau. A few of them are poisonous. The advice is to carry a stick. I do not have a stick and decide it would be dangerous to go into the dense undergrowth to get one and possibly disturb a snake – so I keep to the concrete path with my eyes wide open. Snakes do not usually attack unless provoked so I am very relaxed about snakes on a concrete path.

I didn't see any snakes but back at the Monastery I am told that one day a group of school children came to visit. When they came out of the temple there was such a commotion. They found a snake, a dangerous snake, under their parked bus. No doubt it was as terrified as the children.

In the distance a mountain peak has a frill of cloud around its foothills, like a fluffy collar. I am resting on a boulder staring at a dense grey blanket, listening to the silence, when within seconds it lifts and I can hardly believe my eyes. Far below is a valley with a beautiful lake. Tung Chung valley. As my eyes travel up the mountainside I can see the pinnacle of a temple, just a short distance away from where I'm sitting. I decide to go and look.

Approaching a bend in the path I pause in the mist. I can hear the gongs and the drums and the monks chanting. In that grey, gloomy setting, high in the mountains, it sends shivers down my spine. It is mystical. It is beautiful. It is the Tei Tong Tsai Temple.

The mist is tantalising me. Keeping its secrets from me, blindfolding me with a blanket of greyness, and then suddenly it evaporates to reward me with the most spectacular scenes imaginable. Valleys, ravines, gorges, sparkling lakes, roof tops of distant temples.

I walk back in time for lunch reminding myself that soon I must leave this serenity, this tranquillity. Heavy mist creeps all around the Monastery and I dare not risk being stranded up here in the mountains. If the visibility deteriorates the ferries to the mainland may be cancelled. So I board the minibus at the magnificent triple arches of the temple gates and as it drives away I glance over my shoulder but there is no sign of 'The Precious Lotus Monastery'. It has vanished in the mist.

We rattle and roll and bump our way down through the mountains and woods and hills to arrive at Mui Wo and the ferry. Soon I am in Hong Kong harbour and there she is, neat and sharp and glamorous, the immaculate QE2. She has been painted overall in one day by dozens and dozens and dozens of Chinese workers sitting on planks of wood dangling from ropes!

I hurry to the office and am surprised to find that it has been completely refurbished overnight. A new floor and carpet have been laid. By Chinese workmen, of course.

I grab the envelope I had left on my blotter before I set out for South Lantau. It was addressed to the Social Director and contained information as to where I was going and what to do if I didn't come back. Ship's company are not allowed to sleep off the ship but if I had sought permission it would never have been granted.

A fresh coat of paint for *QE2*. Painted overall in one day – Hong Kong.

And I would never have found that unbelievable mountain paradise of swirling mists, of drums and gongs and rhythmic chants, of incense and freesias perfuming the air, of dogs quarrelling.

I would never have slept in a Buddhist Monastery, I would never have met those gentle Chinese ladies paying tribute to their dear departed... I would never have seen those Chinese horsemen... and I would never have experienced the peace that passeth all understanding. So many memories. I was back safe and sound and no one knew anything about my mystical adventure. I tore up the letter.

Cheung Chau

The following year when the *QE2* tied up at Hong Kong I fixed my sights on Cheung Chau, an island seven miles west of Hong Kong.

We have a lot of embarks but I get as far ahead of the game as I can and organise an overnight bag. Angela, one of our Interpreters asks if she can come with me. She is as exhausted as I am – so off we go to find the early morning ferry.

The journey takes one hour with never a dull moment as junks, sampans, small fishing craft and large general cargo ships jostle around us. Approaching the harbour we can see a whole colony of boat people with an armada of fishing vessels at anchor.

From the moment we step ashore we are caught up in the hustle and bustle of Cheung Chau. Smells of stale fish, smells of burning wood, smells of incense, smells unfamiliar. Stalls line the quayside selling everything from lengths of cloth to fresh mangoes to fish to chickens. You name it – it's here – for sale. The women are so adept with the large knife they wield chopping off the heads of fish, chicken, and other living creatures I can't identify. Down comes that knife! A lot of open-air kitchens fill the air with all manner of good things cooking.

Away from the waterfront the narrow streets are seething with old men and women, young men and women, children running errands, carrying bundles of fresh vegetables, firewood. Young men are doing some welding without eye shields; men are weaving bamboo for baskets, men are pushing trolley loads of fruit and vegetables. As in previous years, east of Bombay everyone is working. Dogs and cats getting into everyone's way.

We approach two very English-looking policemen for directions to the only accommodation on the island. Pine House. After a few wrong turnings down alleyways and side streets we find ourselves on one of the many pathways and are most surprised to see two handsome young men coming towards us. Westerners, in smart suits, collar and ties, carrying briefcases. An incongruous sight. They could have been on their way to a Board Meeting in any modern city in the world.

I think they are just as surprised to see us and stop to chat. They are Mormon missionaries. On an island in the South China Sea! They

Approaching the harbour we can see a whole colony...

know Pine House. It's close by and they lead the way. One of the Americans has a good command of Cantonese and tells the landlady what we want and then they went on their way – I have no idea where to!

We follow her up a tiled, dusty staircase and she shows us some rooms. We decide on a twin-bedded (for security). The bed has no sheets but a thick padded coverlet and four small white pillows. I look under the bed and see what I consider to be the droppings of a small rat or a very large mouse. I decide to say nothing. There is no choice of hotel on this small island. A bird in the hand...

Cheung Chau lies south-east of Lantau Island, a small island a bit bigger than Sark. It is famous for its Bun Festival held every year in May but we are too early. It used to be a pirates' haunt and the cave of the most famous pirate of all, Cheung Po Chai is on this island.

There are no roads, no motor vehicles and it was just wonderful to wander along the broad concrete pathways linking the houses across the island which is quite flat. We find a Temple but can't find the famous pirate's cave.

After lunch – we had quite a language problem as the menus are in Chinese – we go back to the crowded waterfront buzzing with activity. We watch junks being built by lean, sinewy men hammering and scraping and banging. They are sturdy, substantial boats, all timber. Then we hear a band of musicians and see a crowd of excited people in a thick circle near the band. Open air entertainment perhaps, so we go and look.

We stop in our tracks. It is a Buddhist funeral. The coffin is in the shape of a tree trunk, highly polished. Behind it is a small table with dishes of oranges and behind that is the priest in an emerald green surplice and the mourners, all wearing long white robes. They are on their knees, amongst the fruit and fish and vegetable stalls. The principal mourners are wearing white head bands with red or blue emblems. One man carries a large photo of a good-looking middle-aged man.

The waterfront ceremony over they walk in a straggly procession along the quayside and follow a broad concrete path. Four men carry the tree trunk coffin suspended on two poles. We tag along behind, keeping some paces back from the last mourners. The cortège winds along the footpaths for some distance and reaches the burial ground. Digging is still going on and there is much discussion among the mourners.

We sit on a wall to watch the proceedings at the graveside. The priest rings bells, raises his hands and the mourners start walking slowly round the grave. We can only see their heads and shoulders as we are some hundred yards away. Then, to our astonishment, the priest pulls a live chicken out of a carrier bag. In Lincolnshire it would have been described as a Rhode Island Red – a sturdy bird with reddish-brown feathers. The priest holds it high over the grave. We couldn't see what happened to it but we heard no squawks and saw no feathers flying.

Now a fire has been lit and wisps of burnt paper are fluttering away in the wind. After more bustling about a young man takes up a position by the wall not far from us. He is carrying a plastic carrier bag like the bags we get from supermarkets. The mourners take off their white robes and file past him. He gives each one of them something. It looks like a small envelope.

The ceremony over we sit quietly watching as the mourners go on their way. The young man then comes along the path in our direction. We are still sitting on the wall. He delves into his plastic carrier bag and gives each of us an envelope. It contains a coin and a sweet! I still have that coin.

This remarkable incident leaves us both with lots to think about. The colourful procession, the beautifully polished tree trunk coffin has to be seen to be believed and the whole atmosphere is one of celebration and for us to have been acknowledged as surrogate mourners really moves us into another world. A wonderful experience. And no one cried at that funeral.

We have dinner on the waterfront, seafood of course, and then back to Pine House where we crash. I make the bedroom door secure with the usual barricade of chairs and bags and we settle down for the night only to be disturbed by a strange sound that seems to come from under the bed. It is a whirring noise, like a spinning top. It stops and then starts again after a pause. We put the light on to investigate. Then we spot a baby lizard on the wall between the beds. It disappears in a flash and we do not see it or hear it again.

The next morning we set off along the footpaths to explore the other side of the island but there is a lot of reclamation work going on. Diggers and earth-movers and tractors. We need that like a hole in the head. It all looks and sounds horribly familiar so we don't linger. But in spite of that unwelcome activity Cheung Chau preserves a charming old-style way of life. It has been an interesting, peaceful adventure and we return to the ship like giants refreshed ready for a mountain of work again.

Dairen

Cunard made history again the following year during her World Cruise. *QE2*, the largest liner in the world was the first western cruise ship to dock at Dairen in the People's Republic of China. The name is the Japanese version of the Chinese name Ta-lien; it is also called Luta. It sits on the southern edge of the Liaotung peninsular in South Manchuria with North Korea to the east across Korea Bay. To the west is the Gulf of Chihli and mainland China.

Dairen was first developed by the Russians in 1898 as a terminus for the Trans-Siberia railroad and the city was opened to commerce in 1901. The city, along with Port Arthur, was occupied by the Japanese during World War II. And Cunard has found it and brought thousands of cruise passengers to take a look.

Ships are at berth and at anchor and the dockside bustles with

A crowd has congregated outside the dock gates. Welcome to Dairen, China.

activity. A Norwegian cargo vessel is discharging cement. Lorries are being loaded, cranes are clanging. The dock-side is immaculate, not so much as a scrap of paper to be seen. Just a bleak acreage of concrete with grey-garbed workmen in a huddle at the corners of the buildings gazing up at the decadent West portrayed by *QE2*. For as far as the eye can see there are wharves and cranes and dry docks and warehouses and factory chimneys spewing out smoke.

Briefing of passengers here is quite simple and straightforward after the complexity of Canton. All are welcome to take photographs but not in the dock area. We can walk freely in Dairen but must return to the ship by midnight. Two years ago in Canton no one was allowed to leave the hotel and we had to stay in groups with a Chinese Guide – times have changed.

Imagine a large city with broad, tree-lined avenues and NO traffic – just bikes and an occasional lorry or bus. No shops. The sunshine is brilliant but it is bitterly cold. The wind is icy and very strong – 50 mph.

Quite a crowd has congregated outside the dock gates. The adults stand on steps at the back and the children in their brightly coloured padded jackets are at the front gazing at the spectacle of all these strange-looking people from far away spilling into their broad, bare streets, wide enough to accommodate a marching army. Children like to be touched. Everywhere I go they reach for my hands and are reluctant to release their grip. Once again I get the feeling that these children need more cuddling.

On leaving the dock I walk into these wide, deserted streets. There is a well-organised Mission to Seamen. A huge, gaunt building on five floors. In the entrance hall are portraits of the Communist Leaders – Lenin, Marx, Stalin and several I couldn't identify. Mao Tse-tung was missing. The Mission offers all kinds of facilities – a general department store, restaurant, music shop, curiosity shop, Nature Hall with plants, flowers and birds in cages. Sports Hall – billiards, table tennis.

On our second day in port Angela and I go walking in the city. No sooner have we set off than we are surrounded by a group of young Chinese men. They are students at Dairen University and want to practise their English.

'Hullo, how are you? Where would you like to go? We offer China in friendship.' This remarkably tall young man smiles at me.

'Is my intonation good?'

'You say 'How do you do' on greeting and the reply is 'How do you do' – Yes.'

'Which English books do you read?' I ask.

In a chorus they reply 'Dickens.'

And so it goes on. Their incessant questions raining upon us as we wander along the drab, empty streets, past towering, grey buildings that look alike. They are the Export Offices, Police Station, Hotel, Theatre – there is nothing to distinguish one from another. No colour, no paint, no posters.

By now, like the Pied Piper, we have gathered up hordes of children. They are wearing brightly coloured knitted jumpers and the inevitable trousers. Old people stop and stare, young girls giggle in doorways, the young men smile.

There is no public transport but there are a few cars driving along the street.

'Who do the cars belong to?' I ask.

'No one.'

'But they must belong to someone.' I say.

'They are for the people. If anyone needs a car for the day for family business, a wedding, a funeral, they just apply to the appropriate office.'

So that's how it's done!

There are many changes since my visit to Canton two years ago. It is much more relaxed from the administration point of view and we have the freedom of the city. As our group of students said – it is all in friendship for the New China.

So it's back to the ship and back to my desk to tackle the next round of Receptions. But that evening Joe Loss who leads his

Orchestra round the world on the *QE2*, introduces the Chinese people to half a century of Western music in a unique performance in Dairen. It's the first time a Western showband and dance orchestra has appeared in the People's Republic of China. Needless to say he and his Orchestra got them all 'In the Mood.'

Dairen is a fascinating place to visit, tucked away and out of reach of the claws of Western modernisation – for the time being!

This 'invasion' of China by Cunard cruise passengers took place in 1979 and I've described what I saw at that time. Now, tourists go by the plane load every day. The streets are clogged with cars instead of bicycles. The Chinese people wear colour. The young women wear ripped jeans, Gucci shoes and black nail polish. The policy of the 'one child family' is well established. And I cannot believe that that young man is still using a little wooden ladle on a long pole to fill his bucket!

The Three Rivers Gorge is in the process of being dammed and a million Chinese are being relocated. Chek Lap Kok airport occupies the northern part of South Lantau Island. They chopped off the tops of mountains and used the rubble to fill in the sea. Bridges link the islands. And I think of my night at the Po Lin Monastery and the peace and tranquillity I found there.

China will never be the same again.

Japan

Nagasaki

A cold, bright and sunny morning finds us steaming towards Nagasaki set in an amphitheatre cradled by tree smothered mountains on three sides rising in shades of green and brown all around the harbour with tiered houses clinging to the hillsides. A large hawk is hovering over the ship. The hawks would have been here long before the container ships.

As we approach Dejima Pier we can see and hear a brass band on the dockside playing us in. It sets the mood for a happy and relaxed visit. Every port offers its welcome with music and crowds of people. We are within easy walking distance of the town centre and its crooked, winding streets with neat two-storey houses.

I was invited to join the *QE2* Officers' excursion by bus. First we go to the Peace Statue – an enormous bronze figure of a man, 33 feet high, in a powerful and unusual stance. He is a big, muscular man with his eyes closed, his left arm pointing to the sky, sitting on a flat rock, one leg folded across the plinth. Symbolic, full of power, yet denying power with his right arm outstretched in a calming action. The statue was erected in 1955 as an 'expression of sincere desire of the citizens of Nagasaki for everlasting peace in the world'.

Then to the International Cultural Hall, epicentre of the atomic bomb explosion. Rooms are filled with large pictures of the devastation caused. Metal roofs twisted and crumpled like paper. Millstones shattered. In another room we see horrific pictures of the victims of the bomb. It was dropped at 11.02 on 9 August 1945. The second atomic bomb to fall on Japan.

Large photos of mutilated bodies, hideously maimed and burned, skeletons, arms, legs. Unbelievable human suffering. Before the powers that be think of pressing that button, they ought to go first to this

Cultural Hall in Nagasaki. This International Cultural Hall and Peace Statue are not included in the Shore Excursions for passengers who are mainly United States citizens.

We climb endless steps and walk along stone pathways. Waterfall fountains shower us as we wander into the gardens of Glover House to be rewarded by a fantastic view of Nagasaki. The tourist brochure reminds opera lovers of the scene in Puccini's Madame Butterfly where she stands on the hill gazing across this harbour, pining for the return of Pinkerton.

The gardens are surrounded by a thick green hedge with a showy carpet of flowers and plants in tubs. A group of officials each give a short welcome speech and we are then served tea by beautiful Japanese girls in gorgeous kimonos gliding amongst us in their platform-soled flip-flops and white socks. The tea is hot and looks like thick pea soup. It tastes and smells like grass, simply ghastly.

Fortunately I am standing close to that hedge next to a small shrub growing in a tub. With my eyes fixed on the official and listening intently to what he is saying I carefully lower my little tea cup and empty the contents into the tub.

Then it's back to the ship through the hills I had seen when we docked this morning. Crowds of people come to wave as we slip away from the dockside with bands playing, flags flying, streamers streaming and the night sky alive with fireworks.

Yokohama

The first thing I see when I look out of my port hole is a Shell Refinery. There is no escape from refineries and container terminals anywhere in the world. It is wall to wall traffic, spaghetti junctions and flyovers but they don't use their horns so this makes the city reasonably tranquil.

A hundred years ago Yokohama was an insignificant fishing village.

Now, Yokohama is a big, modern booming port for Tokyo just a short distance away and, once again, we dock close to the city centre. The quayside is crowded and every person is taking photos of the *QE2*.

The majority of the people in the streets are wearing Western dress. I wander into a park, dry and arid, then find myself in Chinatown quite by chance. Narrow streets buzzing with life. There are shops, bazaars, street vendors and restaurants festooned with lanterns.

From Chinatown I cross a bridge over shallow muddy waters to a most elegant shopping street, Motomachi. There is no traffic at all here! Fabulous shops displaying gorgeous dresses and suits. Ungaro; Nina Ricci; Yves St Laurent; Christian Dior – exquisite designs in pale blue, pale grey, beige, eau de Nil. How I drool but the price tags are quite beyond me so...

It is an overnight port and although Tokyo is but a short distance away by bullet train I have no appetite for a big, noisy city. I want to escape with an overnight bag if possible so I find the Tourist Office and a most efficient young lady speaking fluent English tells me about a remote island – Oshima. It is accessible by air, practically uninhabited and with just a small fishing village where I will find night accommodation. Now this presents me with a communication problem similar to my South Lantau experience but she solves it by writing a 'Plan' for me. She writes questions in English for which I need answers.

1. I want to go to Oshima and stay in a Pension with meals. One night.

2. I must be back to Yokohama Pier by noon tomorrow.

Under these questions she writes the Japanese equivalent. Hieroglyphics that look like Gregg shorthand gone wrong.

Kinkyori Airways has flights to Oshima Island. She gives me a copy of the timetable but it is meaningless apart from the numbers denoting flight and departure times. Then I realise just what I am getting myself into. It is highly unlikely that I will find an English-speaking fisherman on this remote island! That familiar mini-terror seizes me, momentarily. But I am determined and the more I think about visiting this remote island, the more enthusiastic I become, so armed with information about flights and currency I return to the ship to prepare my bag.

Striding across the Park I meet a young, white man. He stops and we chat. In these distant places it is quite natural to speak to complete strangers. In fact you would never pass one without a word. I think it's a kind of anchorage. A security of identity. This young man is Canadian working at the Embassy in Yokohama. Learning Japanese. It has taken two years and has been a terrific slog. I can believe him after my experience in the Tour Office I had just left. The only thing I could understand was the numbers.

Back on board I am staggered to learn that the embark has gone up from 127 to 420 passengers so that's the end of my dream of Oshima. There is not the remotest chance of getting away. I have to get cracking on the organisation for the Captain's Reception. It's not easy because of the triple-barrelled names – Mr Hu Flung Dung or simply Mr Ng.

Kagoshima

Overnight we retrace our wake along the Pacific coast of Japan to Kagoshima where we get a reception to end all receptions. It is spectacular! The dockside is packed. More than two hundred men, women and children in colourful costumes are here to welcome us with flags and pompoms. Dozens of horses bedecked with flowers parade on the quay. A sight to remember at eight o'clock in the morning. Above, a helicopter trails a message of welcome for the *QE2*.

This is another 'inaugural' port – so I am busy with plans for the official reception but manage to get down the gangway after lunch. Once again, I find elegant shops full of elegant clothes. The children, speaking excellent English, mob me. So inquisitive, so curious – simply delightful.

On one street, not far from the dock on the pavement in the open air, smart young men and women sit at a long trestle table covered with a white cloth piled high with street maps and brochures. They are bombarded with questions from the passengers and deal with them all courteously and with great good humour. It is an open air Information Desk. How's that for good Public Relations?

With such a short time in port we often miss some of the most important Festival Events – such as the Sacred Palanquins, the June Lamp Festival, the Umbrella Burning Festival and many more but we must be thankful. These people give us such a spontaneous welcome and do everything to make our stay memorable.

The Mayor of Kagoshima has arranged for every passenger and crew member to receive a little souvenir of our visit. These souvenirs (more than 2,000) are brought on board in dozens and dozens of large cartons and distributed to the different Departments who deliver the gift to every passenger and crew member. I receive a box containing an exquisite model of a Japanese doll in a kimono.

Kagoshima is beautiful and a world away from the traffic jams of Yokohama and Tokyo. There are parks and flowers and temples and volcanic mountains in the distance but it is time to sail away from these islands on the other side of the world.

Passengers and as many of the ship's company who are not on duty, go on deck for departure from port. It is thrilling and sad and happy, such a scale of mixed emotions. And if we thought our welcome to Kagoshima surpassed all we had ever seen, another surprise came when we left at eleven o'clock that evening.

Hundreds and hundreds and hundreds of men, women and children line the quayside, each one carrying a lighted lantern. As we sail away the swaying lights become smaller and smaller until we are staring at a myriad of diamond pins on a huge, black velvet curtain. A truly fantastic sight. Unforgettable.

Tristan da Cunha

Where is it? Well, find an atlas, find South Africa, find Cape Town and go due west – slowly or you will miss it – and there you will see these lonely specks of land sitting in splendid isolation in the middle of the South Atlantic. I say 'they' because Tristan da Cunha is one of a group of three volcanic islands – the others are Inaccessible and Nightingale, both uninhabited.

Inaccessible is about twenty miles from Tristan da Cunha. It has cliffs 1,000 feet high. There are narrow fringes of beach at the base of the cliffs in some places. Landing is possible but only in small boats in favourable weather.

Nightingale, the smallest and southernmost island, is 10 miles from Inaccessible and 25 miles from Tristan da Cunha. Landing can

QE2 approaching Tristan da Cunha, South Atlantic.

be made under suitable conditions by leaping on to a rocky platform as the swell raises the boat to its level! Canvas boats are then hauled on to the rocks.

The Portuguese, led by Admiral Tristan da Cunha, were the first to find these 'black blobs' in the ocean in 1506. Tristan da Cunha is the largest and northernmost and is roughly circular. Winds are generally strong and variable. The islands have been under British control since 1816 when a garrison of soldiers was stationed here to prevent its use by privateers. The present settlers are descendants from shipwrecked sailors, settlers of European extraction and women from St Helena.

We steam across the South Atlantic Ocean scanning the vast horizon for that small black blob. The islands materialise mid-morning and excitement grows as the small black blob becomes a large black blob.

From a distance the island looks bleak and barren but as we get closer we can see that the sand and rock on the beach are black. There are many kinds of grasses and ferns and an island tree (*Phylica nitida*). A frill of lowlands skirts around the edge of the shoreline which is fresh and green with wooded slopes giving way to high peaks of rock.

Edinburgh is a neat cluster of well-built houses in a green paddock completely sheltered under the 6,700 foot peak. A heavy swell crashes on to the rocks rising sheer from the sea. Through binoculars I can see neat paddocks with cows grazing. A well-made road winds through the settlement. I can see fuel tanks close by the road. A dog running across a meadow. Cloud drifts over the volcanic peak forming an umbrella over the island in an otherwise clear sky.

The islanders are completely self-supporting and receive no aid from the UK except for specific projects. There is no income tax. They make their own furniture, beds, cupboards. They have cows and the bull is changed every few years. They have chickens and grow potatoes and other vegetables. There is a crayfish factory on the quayside. Water is from the mountain streams and they generate their own electricity which is expensive. There is a Government Guest House where visitors can stay. Cape Town is their nearest shopping centre!

There is no shore leave for passengers or crew but two of our Radio Officers go ashore to repair the transmitter.

The islanders are invited on board and they come out to the *QE2* in their own motor boats. A tea party has been arranged for all the children (63) in the Q4 Room. Jellies, cakes, party games and a present for every child. They are very well-mannered but rather shy.

The parents, grandparents and children wander around the decks and into the Double Down Room and Queen's Room where the passengers mingle with them, taking photographs and chatting and learning about their way of life on a tiny patch of land about forty square miles in the middle of an ocean.

Postage stamps for our inaugural visit are the top priority. Official *QE2* First Day covers are spectacular with stamps measuring five inches by two inches, franked 'Tristan da Cunha – South Atlantic – Paquebot' and autographed by the islanders. Ten thousand Tristan postage stamps were sold in less than two hours!

I meet the girls selling stamps – two of them, Susan and Julie Green, are cousins. Some are brunettes with dark eyes. Some are blue-eyed blondes but the Mediterranean type is dominant. All speak English, some with a South African accent. I also meet Mr and Mrs Ben Claxton, the Deputy Administrator and his wife, both from England.

The other souvenir I bring home is 'a genuine piece of volcanic rock from the remotest inhabited island in the world'. The volcano erupted in October 1961 and all the inhabitants were evacuated to England until 1963.

But it's time to go and these charming, gentle families scramble into their boats. Everyone wears a lifejacket for the short journey. Landing is difficult with that unpredictable swell and so we watch and wave as they head back to the peace and seclusion of their island.

I stay on deck as we sail away, the big black blob becoming a small black blob again then I go back to the office to make more plans for champagne and caviar and feel a profound envy for these people who can watch the sun rise and set over a limitless horizon, who can borrow a tractor when they need one, who can invite a neighbour to help to rebuild a shed, who can fish in crystal waters, who can breathe unpolluted air and who know how to care for their neighbour and their neighbour's children on one of the loneliest islands in the world, free from the contagious frenzy of power and greed.

I would have given anything to tune in to their conversation over supper that evening. What could they have thought of it all? Probably felt quite sorry for us!

A day I will never forget.

South Africa

Cape Town

There are very high winds as we approach Cape Town and waves are crashing on to the distant beach. Looking through binoculars I can see mountains rising from the sea and a ridge of trees running the entire length of the summit – The Lion. A small aircraft comes to say 'hello'– I think. It has two torpedo-shaped things on the wing tips! It doesn't stay and then a helicopter comes spluttering through the sky bringing the Pilot and Immigration officials to the *QE2*.

I have a lot of work to do but I can't wait to get ashore. The high winds persist and create a veritable dust storm in the dock area, so open to the sea. Just a short distance from the ship there is a steam engine on its own, no wagons. Three men in khaki uniforms and peaked caps are standing on its bumpers at the front staring at the ship. Uncharacteristically, I do not ask them what they are doing – they are both armed! But it's just a steam engine. Who would want to steal it? I pick up a small lump of coal near the railway tracks. That is more than I can do in Southampton Docks. Steam engines and railway tracks are alive and well here in South Africa. I brought the piece of coal home with me.

A red double-decker bus with open top and a large banner 'Welcome to QE2' is waiting to take passengers and crew to the city centre. Cape Town is captivating. Spacious, uncluttered wide streets, no sense of crowding with a great sense of freedom. And I love the wind. It is in command here along with the majestic Table Mountain – breathtaking in its solidarity.

The shops are quiet and the assistants so polite. A young, bronzed man in shorts with the right leg amputated just below the knee is making great strides on crutches. I don't know why this should have found its way into my diary notes. Perhaps it's because he is young and handsome, perhaps the unfairness of it jars on the harmony of everything around me. Perhaps a reminder that all things are not equal in the world, certainly not here. I wander into a flower market, such a kaleidoscope of colour.

This beautiful spacious city is so clean and the strong wind is so powerful with Table Mountain dominating the whole scene. I just walk the streets in a trance and feel very elated and happy. The wind energises me, makes me sing.

I find the Cape Town National Gallery and see an Exhibition of English landscapes. Yes, another Art Gallery but you can skip it. One painting in particular interests me. 'The Melton Hunt – the brook under Tilton on the Hill' painted by J. Ferneley, Snr (1782 – 1860) I was born in the village of Holwell, two miles from Melton Mowbray so I am intrigued to see a painting of my native land so far away from home. My mother often took us, my two sisters and brother, to see the Quorn Hunt when they met. We were only very small but I can remember the scything legs of big horses ridden by heavy, meaty men with purple faces wearing red jackets (hunting pink of course). To find a picture of the Quorn Hunt at Melton Mowbray in South Africa is bordering on the bizarre.

The next morning I have finished my work by half past ten, packed an overnight bag and go to find the railway station.

It is a Victorian building with a dome of a ceiling and acres of concourse, with very few people about. On either side are rows and rows of ticket offices with clerks sitting behind the glass-fronted counters. I have no idea where to go but I need to get away from the ship to recharge the batteries and I do not want to meet any passengers. I know where all the tours are going so looked for a destination that does not feature in our excursion brochures. I scan the Departure Board. Row upon row of unfamiliar places. Choose one. Stellenbosch had a good ring about it so I go up to one of the windows.

'Can I get to Stellenbosch in a day?' I ask.

'Yes.' The young man doesn't look up from his papers.

'Are there hotels there?'

'Yes.' Now he notices me.

'Is it tranquil?' My routine question.

'Yes. No trouble at all.'

I buy a return ticket and find the platform and the train. It's a diesel. I step on board only to be turned off immediately. I didn't notice the sign above the entrance to that compartment. Blacks only. So I wander along the platform until I find a compartment in which I can travel and we are soon on our way winding through the outskirts of Cape Town, leaving behind the power lines and railway tracks and scrapyards and shanty towns to meander through a pleasant, peaceful countryside.

The train arrives at Stellenbosch station one hour later. It has a narrow platform, a wooden building and a goods yard. One train is loaded with timber. That's it. Not a soul is arriving or departing. Just me.

I walk along broad, tree-lined streets with neat two-storey white houses, shuttered windows, bright well-kept gardens until I come to the main drag. From across the street I study Hotel Coutzenburg. Looks all right to me so I step inside. The hotel is three hundred years old, solid and permanent, clean, comfortable and lived in. Not a hint of plastic to be seen.

My room is light and airy with a verandah. I decide it is quite safe to sleep with the French windows open and that night I lay in my bed staring up at the African night sky full of stars. I breathed the purest pine-scented air and slept the sleep of queens.

The next morning I went to explore. The air is like champagne, the sun sparkles on everything and the sky cannot be contained. I hear again the African sounds – the crickets, the screech of birds high in the trees, the lazy rhythm of everyday life. The streets of Stellenbosch are lined with oak trees and open channels of water from the River Eerste.

It is the oldest town in South Africa after Cape Town, founded in 1679 by the Governor Simon van der Stel. The beautiful Cape Dutch houses are neat and content in their surroundings and maintain the superiority inherited from their affluent merchant forebears who had them built.

Such was my ignorance that I had never heard of Stellenbosch until I walked into Cape Town railway station. I didn't realise that it is the centre of a wine state. It lies in a valley surrounded by pine forests and mountain ranges. I can see many vineyards.

Stellenbosch is spotlessly clean. There is not a scrap of rubbish and not a soft drink can to be seen.

I visit the Museum – Grosvenor House. Sorry about all these Museums and Art Galleries – to me a chance of a life time! A patrician town house maintained in the manner to which it was born. It is an early Cape town house of two storeys with a flat roof. Building began in 1782 by Christian Ludolph Neethling who was employed by the Dutch East India Company as secretary to the Council of Justice in Cape Town. It reached its present appearance in about 1803 when the Collins family lived there. Wooden shutters protect sash windows and tubs of flowers form a guard of honour along the pavement. At the rear there are gardens, sun dials, secluded corners. It was established as a local history museum in 1962.

After the hustle and bustle of cocktail parties night after night after night and dealing with passenger problems I am in another world. What are these passenger problems I keep mentioning? Well, it's usually personality conflict and the problem some men have with the excess of female passengers on board. For instance, an elderly German tells me that he has two awful women at his table. Man eaters! He pretends he doesn't speak English and he also pretends to be deaf, thus escaping practically unscathed but he has to be on guard all the time. The solution would have been to change his table but the ship is full to capacity – no chance. On the other side of that coin I have the ladies beseeching me to introduce them to men!

And there is another incident which is causing quite a problem. A shabbily dressed man in his fifties embarked at Sydney and started agitating immediately for a better cabin. He wanders around the ship pestering women to buy opals. He has a pocket full of them. What are we going to do about this man who is a fully paid up passenger, making a big nuisance of himself? There are ways and means. On arrival at the next port Customs fine him $4,000 for smuggling and deport him to Australia.

But I am wandering. Where were we? Stellenbosch. Beautiful, clean and colourful. There is so much space in Africa. The tempo is relaxed. The sky is huge and so blue, the trees are so green, the colour of the ladies' dresses so vivid. Everything seems in excess of beauty.

But duty calls. I must leave. So I stroll back to the little wooden building at the side of the railway track and wait for the train to Cape Town, thirty-one miles away.

We have a spectacular Carnival Show in the Double Down Room before sailing. A troupe of about twenty men and children from the Malay district of Cape Town, a strange mixture racially whose ancestry goes back to the Hottentots. They are wearing vivid suits of purple, yellow, orange – with lots of glitter. They bring the ship to life with such a splash of colour, such rhythms. Two small boys, probably six or seven years old, just about steal the show. They wear white suits and sing completely out of tune but they charm the passengers out of their seats.

Soon I am back into the routine, tramping the metal decks, breathing through gills again and ploughing into the manifest of South African embarks but I am feeling very relaxed and refreshed – and smug. Once again I've pulled it off. I have slept away from the ship and not a soul knows about it!

Sailing is delayed because of that notorious wind and we are unable to leave harbour until 4a.m. Then we head for the Cape of Good Hope and Durban.

Durban

We arrive at two o'clock in the afternoon – late. I manage a walk ashore at half past four. Durban is a huge, sprawling city and a busy port. At first sight – dull. Garages and cinemas.

But my time to explore is limited so my impression of Durban may be distorted. Old Colonial buildings such as the Local History Museum and the Library – mellow old buildings almost dwarfed by the ugly skyscraper blocks of offices and flats. So what's new?

Durban is the hub of South Africa's Zulu heartland and tonight in the Double Down Room we have a display of tribal dancing by a group of Zulu warriors. About sixty men wearing ornate necklets and animal skins around their waists. Feathered headdresses waft with every movement and the white armlets and leggings of white brushed goat hair synchronise the rhythms. The warriors enter in two files from either side of the stage into the centre of the dance floor chanting and stamping and waving shields and spears to the beat of extremely powerful drums.

There are 12 musicians. Some are banging two pieces of wood together. Some are drummers. Some are blowing through the tips of large spiral horns. They are Kudu horns. They make a fantastic siren of noise throughout the ship which vibrates as they stamp and whistle. The musicians are younger than the dancers.

The Chief stands in front of the group of men who perform in rows and circles and at a given point he blows a whistle to change the tempo. These African rhythms touch some primordial chord in me – I experienced the same frisson in Haiti – and the spectacle seems to revitalise the passengers after their day of sightseeing. I am impressed with the physical power of these strong men, performing as their forebears must have performed through the centuries. And to think they want to build supermarkets and highways across Africa! Well, they can and will but I can never see this power of tribal ritual ever being destroyed. It is bred in the bone. So deep and ageless and powerful.

We sail away in a blaze of ships' sirens and trail of streamers. Crowds of people watching as usual and a Pipe Band gives us a stirring send-off, marching and counter-marching on the dock-side. We slip past the backdrop of the heavily wooded shore with oil refineries and cargo ships relaxing after the rigours of the oceans. Soon we are clear of the harbour and the skirl of the pipes fades to a whisper in the breeze

Mombasa Kenya

I'm going to tell you about this brief visit to Mombasa because of an unusual and inexplicable experience in my many visits ashore.

The dock area is a shambles. Shacks and heaps of stinking rubbish, scruffy dogs, barefoot children. So I walk into town and find the Tourist Office. I would be lost without the Tourist Offices around the world. They provide most of my information and always a map. I had earmarked Nakuru in the Great Rift Valley for a visit but after gleaning more information it's clearly a non-starter. It is 97 miles north-west of Nairobi. Out of the question. So think again. The Tsavo National Park is 65 miles from Mombasa – again too far.

What about a bus to Shemba Hills? – the heat in Mombasa is searing. There is no transport to Shemba Hills. But I did find a bus to Ukundu, south of Mombasa along a well-maintained coast road bordered by sandy beaches protected by coral reefs and palm trees. The aquamarine sea with its white frilly petticoat flirts with the pale sand and, on the other side, way into the hinterland for as far as the eye can see, is a thick rich belt of green woods and flat savanna in the distance.

Ukunda is just a road-side stop really. A huddle of small huts and street stalls. A narrow gravel drive leads to a Club-Hotel amongst the trees. There seems to be nothing else at Ukunda so I decide to go and look at this sophisticated Club-Hotel. It is a settlement of luxurious, air-conditioned bungalows, surrounded by acres of tropical park full of exotic flowers. It has its own beach and reefs and looks very peaceful and inviting.

I have my overnight bag with me but looking around this playground for the rich and the famous there is nothing but dark eyes watching me. Groups of young men lolling around the reception area, in the courtyard, at the back of a low wall next to the outbuildings, near the bungalows.

I wander into the open lobby and the attractive young receptionist explains that there is accommodation available in a bungalow. I glance around the lounge and there is not a visitor or guest to be seen. Not a chink of a cup or glass can be heard, not a barman to be seen, nor a waiter. No one. There is not a sound. Not even from those youths outside.

They don't seem to be doing anything. They aren't even talking to each other. Their eyes are on me. Alarm bells ring in the far reaches of my mind. Who are these young men? They are clean and smartly dressed, not urchins demanding 'one dollar please'. Perhaps they are employed here but if so why aren't they working? Instinct tells me to go away. I thank the receptionist and leave this phantom Club-Hotel.

I retrace my steps along the gravel drive. Some men and women are waiting on the opposite side of the road so I cross over and ask about the bus to Mombasa. They don't speak English but recognised the word 'Mombasa' and nod and smile. Lucky me.

We didn't have to wait long. A minibus swooshes to a halt in a cloud of red dust. It's already quite full but everyone scrambles on board. I wait until last and find a seat between two plump African ladies. Off we go.

They are all talking at the same time at the tops of their voices and it sounds as if everyone knows everyone. We stop from time to time and more people squeeze on. By now it is standing room only but still they are all talking to each other at the same time with animated voices. No doubt it's a perfectly normal exchange but alien to my ears, it sounds like a heated argument. I use local transport a lot and I am always amazed how acceptable I am on their buses. I am the only white skin to be seen but nobody bats an eyelid and I always get a smile.

At last we are wending our way through the streets of Mombasa and it's a relief when the people begin to pour off the bus. It's very hot and stuffy and I am a grease spot. Soon I recognise the main drag and find the Castle Hotel where I collapse in the cool Lounge with afternoon tea.

This is the only time I have ever sensed danger on my excursions. As I drink my tea I keep thinking about those youths at the posh Club-Hotel at Ukunda. There must have been a dozen or more. One of my shipmates, Patti Graham and I went on safari, just the two of us, petite, pale-skinned, blue-eyed blondes – driving hundreds of miles in a Toyota right through Malawi, Uganda, Rhodesia (now Zimbabwe) and the Africans we met were smiling, talkative, friendly people. These youths acted completely out of character. No smiles, no chats. They just stared. No doubt they were harmless and a white woman with a pale skin does have some freak value. But my instinct is never wrong and I disregard it at my peril.

Mombasa is a cultural mix of Africans, Asians, Arabs and Portuguese with mosques, temples, Anglican and Roman Catholic cathedrals but there is no time for sightseeing. I finish my tea. Time to go.

The Seychelles

The *QE2* dropped anchor off Victoria early in the morning and we are here for the day. This is a launch port but the sea is calm and we get all the passengers ashore safely. There are parties to organise, invitations to sort but looking out on that tropical paradise from the Boat Deck I know I must go ashore if only for a few hours so, as promised, I made contact with Lou, one of our Terrible Ten, at mid-day.

The launch broke down, just our rotten luck with such limited time, but we eventually step ashore and find a taxi. English and French are the official languages and a Creole patois is spoken. Henry, (yes, and he is barefoot!) our driver, speaks good English. We explain that we want to get away from Mahé streets and shops and people and we are soon being led along rough tracks through dense foliage.

He is very knowledgeable and able to identify the flowers and ferns and trees and orchids and bougainvillea and hibiscus and frangipani. There are pitcher plants which I had first seen in Sabah. He points out a number of poisonous plants. Often it is just the berries or fruits that are poisonous but he tells us that all parts of the strychnine tree are poisonous and he wants to find one for us but we had no luck.

We follow him along rough tracks through dense foliage and he pauses at a tree with a thick, rugged brown trunk. He pulls out a knife (!) scoring the bark with the blade several times. It oozes red sap. The dragon's blood tree.

A little further along, in dense undergrowth, he points out a wild pineapple. Its spikes are about four feet tall but the fruit is smaller and more elongated than the ones we see in our shops.

He names the birds we see flitting through the trees and undergrowth. The mahte, black and yellow and not unlike our jay but smaller. The toutrail like a miniature pigeon. The cardinal is small, red and quite beautiful. The feather tail is a white seabird with a long, long tail, very slender.

The first Europeans landed in the Seychelles in the 17th and 18th centuries and they have left striking accounts of the beauty of the forests that once covered the islands, but the forests are no more. They were felled for housing by the early settlers and for their sailing ships and timber for export.

Before the settlers arrived the isolation of these fragments of land sprinkled across the Indian Ocean allowed a unique variety of plants and animals to develop. The lush green vegetation is unruly, wild and undisturbed by humans. Thick clumps of palms, tall saplings and wise old trees with gnarled and knotted trunks watch over the new growth.

The Government's policy statement on the development of tourism in the Seychelles emphasises the overriding need to protect the natural beauty of the islands and the policy seems to be working. Visitor Passes are granted and are valid initially for one month. Camping is not allowed. Nude bathing is not acceptable in the Seychelles.

Henry wants to take us to see red bananas on the other side of the island but we have no time and must get back to work.

There is a long queue for the launch at the landing stage but we make it in time and I am soon bent over a pile of invitation cards again but my mind is elsewhere.

There is little wonder that the Seychelles is one of the most popular honeymoon destinations for Westerners. There are 92 islands. Time passes slowly here.

Djibouti

From the beauty of the Seychelles we sailed north to the capital of the republic of Somalia, Djibouti, formerly a French protectorate. It is a refuelling and supply station for shipping and the only local significant industry is the production of salt from the sea. But there are dates, fruit and vegetables.

We are homeward bound now and although we are not yet in the Mediterranean, pressure of work is building. Cocktail parties are still being organised but end of voyage papers have to be thought about. I do go ashore for half an hour.

It must be one of the hottest places on earth and what I saw of Djibouti was broken down and shabby. The dock area is a dusty rubbish heap. There are more interesting places to visit but I have no time to see its white buildings, old and modern, and its laurel avenues. Neither could I get to the camel market.

We sail at six o'clock and there is no cocktail party so I go on deck and enjoy the stillness of the night.

Next morning we are sailing through the calm blue waters of the Red Sea. It is much wider than I imagined with no land in sight on either side. As we approach the Suez Canal I can see a few settlements along the banks but my field of vision is filled with the rugged mountainous terrain beyond the timeless desert sands. Not a soul in sight.

The air is crystal clear, the desert serene, the sky cloudless and later that evening a golden orb changes to orange then filters into red, torching the desert sand before it slips away.

There are many images throughout the world cruises that stay with me but the transit of the Red Sea is one of the most graphic. Perhaps it's the stark simplicity of the desert and the harmonious blending of colours – beige, gold, sepia – and the universal space. Albert Camus wrote: 'Individuals grow old and lonely and their pathetic little preoccupations are out of all proportion to the sea and desert...'

QE2 approaches the Suez Canal – nearly home.

From Port Suez we steam up the coast to Haifa in Israel. Most of us are now in familiar waters in the Mediterranean. The days are racing by and excitement is rising. There is a buzz throughout the ship.

That malady, geographical indigestion, continues to manifest itself and I need time to absorb the sights and sounds and music and colour and reflect on the interesting people that I meet in their natural environment, leading lives undreamed of in the Western world.

All those dozens of ports, all those different countries. All those thousands of nautical miles, across all those magical oceans. I remember my walk in the Balinese jungle. Those gentle ladies sitting so quietly on the roadside with their hand-made wares in Tonga. Hobart, Tasmania and the fishermen. China... my stay in the Buddhist Monastery, the lizard on the wall of the bedroom in Cheung Chau. The Chinese Opera, the Cages in Bombay... The little boy scooping water on to the back of the water buffalo. The dockside farewells – in particular all those swaying lanterns as we left Kagoshima. And Sydney was unforgettable.

They are all there, the memories, filed away to be recalled by a chance remark, a photo, a piece of music, a sunset...

There are other landmarks etched in my memory. Thought-provoking. The British influence is noticeable all round the world. Our Parliamentary system, postal system, Civil Service. All those British-built railways and tarmac roads. All those statues and gardens in honour of Queen Victoria. The parades and massed bands I saw have the unmistakable hallmark of Sandhurst... Cranwell...

We have left our mark in many places – but I'm sorry that we stole so many statues and artefacts and sacred objects. We should not have done that.

And all those War Memorials to men and women in countries as far apart as Sri Lanka and Brazil and Papua New Guinea. Men and women who helped to fight our battles and secure the freedom we enjoy today. All that loss of life, the sacrifice for our liberty and here we are in the twenty-first century with that hard fought and costly freedom being threatened.

These oceans we have sailed were once navigated by the explorers in wooden sailing ships with no modern technology, no radar, no radio, no satellite connection. They sailed with only the wind and stars to guide them.

Pirates earned their living plundering, burning and killing. Now the *QE2*, sleek and sophisticated, with all her high-tech. equipment, takes us across the oceans effortlessly and in great comfort.

Armadas of gigantic cruise ships are sailing and more and more are under construction. These modern liners are not so aesthetically pleasing in profile as the classic generation. They look like chunks of apartment blocks floating in the ocean and heaven help them in a Force 10 gale! But President Tito was right... To survive we must change with the times. Now we have *Queen Mary 2*, sailing the oceans of the world. 151,400 tons – our beloved *Queen Mary* was a mere 81,000 tons! And the *QE2* is no longer the largest liner in the world.

So I discovered what was beyond that lonely farm and Grantham.

There was a world of much wealth and extravagance on board those elegant liners and on shore such abject poverty. As I trawl through my notes and diaries of more than twenty years ago I realise that we are all now in a different world with the threat of violence wherever we go.

The greatest sadness is that few lessons have been learned and we are still sucked into wars, devouring the young and old – we never learn. Another sadness is that the poverty I saw in many countries grinds on today.

Now I must finish the reports, balance the books, collate the files and documents. We are nearly home and I've got The Channels and I'm longing to make myself some tea. Tea that tastes nothing like tea anywhere in the world.

At last, there is the silence and solitude in my flat. The United Kingdom seems very much the same as when I left it. But it is spring and the gardens are full of daffodils and tulips. 'Oh to be in England...'

Dignity

(in the foothills of Mount Kinabalu, Sabah)

White man looks at her
    And walks away.

She sits on a table in a hut
    Grinding something
    Slowly
    With dignity.

    Now white man brings woman
    They stare.
Transparent, glassy eyes
    Wonder.

The hut is cool, tranquil.
    Outside
    Bright green trees
    Watch.

    She is old, old
    Yet she fears nothing
    As she grinds
    Red nuts.

    She has no teeth
    But needs the dust
    To ease her pains.

    She is old, old
    With dignity

Muriel Arnold